Simple Vegetarian Cooking

INDIAN STYLE

Simple Vegetarian Cooking

INDIAN STYLE

Shanka Dasa

YOGESVARA PRESS

First edition: First printing, 2010;
Second printing, 2010

Contact information:
Shanka Dasa
17306 NW 112th Blvd.
Alachua, FL 32615, USA
sankadas2002@yahoo.com

Published by Yogesvara Press
Printed in the United States of America

Cover photo:
©Ryan Carter / istockphoto.com

Back cover photo:
©Simon Whitehead/ istockphoto.com

Book design:
Yamaraja Dasa

ISBN 978-1-4507-0310-9

Contents

Dedicated to my spiritual master
HIS DIVINE GRACE A. C. BHAKTIVEDANTA
SWAMI PRABHUPADA
Founder/Acharya of the International Society
for Krishna Consciousness

Introduction and
The Art of Making Ghee

There has always been a great demand for very tasty and easy-to-prepare vegetarian dishes. By the mercy of the Lord, I was able to stay in India for five years. During that time I visited many families in different states, learning how to prepare many traditional dishes. The recipes in this book, and their combinations from the various catagories, provide the ideal vitamin/protein balance for the human diet.

Ghee is clarified butter. It is included in many of the recipes in this book and is used for frying spices, and deep-frying vegetables and savories. This wonderful cooking medium is obtained by the following process: Place a pound or more of unsalted butter in a large saucepan or thick-bottomed pot. Melt and bring to a boil. It will begin foaming. Reduce heat to a soft boil, stirring occasionally to avoid burning. Boil until the butter is clear and all impurities have fallen to the bottom of the pan. Let cool for 20 minutes, then pour carefully through a clean cheese cloth, leaving the impurities in the pan. The fragrant golden liquid that results is called *ghee*.

Some helpful hints:

You can use frozen peas instead of fresh peas (remember to rinse first).

If basmati rice is used, use 1⅔ cups of water per cup of rice.

If curry leaves are not available, they can be left out.

If you cannot find coriander leaves (cilantro), you can substitute them with parsley leaves. However, use less, as they tend to be a little bitter.

Use 1 tablespoon of lemon juice for 2 cups of boiling milk for making curds. Make sure milk is boiling before adding juice (or citric acid—a pinch per cup).

Enjoy!

Dal
(Bean Soups)

Green Mung Dal

1 cup mung dal, split
1 green chili, finely chopped
2 tablespoons ghee
1-inch piece ginger root, grated
pinch of asafetida
1 teaspoon cumin seeds
½ teaspoon turmeric powder
salt to taste

Wash *dal* 3 times. Soak in 8 cups water for 1 hour. In saucepan, heat 1 tablespoon ghee. Add ginger and chili. Fry lightly. Add *dal,* soaking water, and turmeric powder. Cook till *dal* is almost done. Heat remaining ghee. Add cumin and asafetida. When color changes, add to *dal* with salt. Cook till soft. You can use an egg beater or a blender to make it smooth. If too pasty, add more water. Serves 6–7.

Green Mung Dal With White Radish

1 cup mung dal, split
¼ cup chopped radish, plus leaves
½ teaspoon turmeric powder
2 tablespoons ghee

1-inch piece ginger root, grated
1 teaspoon cumin seeds
½ teaspoon cumin powder
pinch of asafetida
chili powder to taste
salt to taste

Wash *dal* 3 times. Soak in 8 cups water for 1 hour. In saucepan, cook in same water with turmeric till soft. Add radish and more water if necessary, and cook till *dal* is very soft. Remove from heat. In frying pan, heat ghee. Add cumin seeds, asafetida, and ginger. When color changes, add chili powder, and salt. Cook briefly. Add to *dal*. Mix well. Cook 5 minutes. You can use an egg beater to make it smooth. If too pasty, add more water. Serves 6–7.

Green Mung Dal with Spinach

1 cup mung dal, split
2 cups spinach, finely chopped
2 tomatoes, sliced
2 tablespoons ghee
1 green chili, finely chopped
1 teaspoon cumin seeds
½ teaspoon mustard seeds
½ teaspoon garam masala
salt to taste

Wash *dal* and soak for 1 hour in 4 cups water. In saucepan, cook in same water with salt, turmeric, and *garam masala* till soft and dry. Set aside. In skillet, heat ghee. Add cumin seeds and mustard seeds. When popping stops, add chilis and ginger. Fry briefly. Add spinach and salt, and mix well. Cook till dry and soft. Pour *dal* on top. Garnish with sliced tomato. Optional garnishes: grated coconut or coriander leaves. Serves 5–6.

Green Mung Dal Curry

1 cup mung dal, whole
1 cup buttermilk
3 tablespoons ghee
1 tablespoon chickpea flour
2 green chilis, finely chopped
½-inch piece ginger root, grated
a few neem leaves
1 teaspoon turbinado sugar
1 teaspoon cumin seeds
½ teaspoon turmeric powder
pinch of asafetida
handful of coriander leaves
salt to taste

Wash *dal* 3 times and soak overnight. Put in muslin cloth and hang till sprouted, washing occasionally. In saucepan, heat ghee. Add cumin seeds and asafetida and fry briefly. Add chilis and ginger. When brown, add chickpea flour. Mix well. Add sprouted *dal,* turmeric, neem leaves, and salt and fry briefly. Add 3 cups water. When almost done, add buttermilk. Cook till soft. Add 1 cup water to make sure *dal* is liquidy. Garnish with coriander leaves. Serves 5–6.

Yellow Mung Dal

1 cup mung dal, split
1 green chili, finely chopped
2 tablespoons ghee

1 teaspoon cumin seeds
½ teaspoon mustard seeds
pinch of asafetida
½ teaspoon turmeric
1 teaspoon garam masala
1 teaspoon cumin powder
handful of coriander leaves
salt to taste

Wash *dal* 3 times and soak in 8 cups water for 1 hour. In saucepan, cook in same water till *dal* starts breaking down. Add turmeric, salt, cumin powder, and *garam masala*. Reduce to low heat. In frying pan, heat ghee. Add cumin seeds, mustard seeds, and asafetida. When popping stops, add chili and ginger. Fry briefly. Add to *dal*. Mix well. Cook 3–5 minutes. Mix in coriander leaves. If too pasty or dry, add more water. Serves 6–7.

Yellow Mung Dal With Mixed Vegetables

1½ cups mung dal, split
1½ cups mixed vegetables,
     cut into small pieces
½-inch piece ginger root, grated
3 tablespoons ghee
1 teaspoon cumin seeds
½ teaspoon mustard seeds
1 teaspoon turmeric powder
½ teaspoon crushed red chilis
handful of coriander leaves
salt to taste

Wash *dal* 3 times. Soak overnight in 5 cups water. Drain. In saucepan, heat ghee. Add cumin seeds, mustard seeds, and red chilis. When popping stops, add ginger, turmeric, and salt. Fry briefly. Add vegetables and *dal*. Cook till dry. Add enough water to cover mixture by 1 inch. Mix well. Cover and cook on low flame till *dal* is broken down. Mix in coriander leaves. If too pasty, mix in more water. Serves 6–7.

Yellow Mung Dal & Coconut

> *1 cup mung dal, split*
> *1 cup grated coconut*
> *½-inch piece ginger root, grated*
> *2 bay leaves*
> *3 tablespoons ghee*
> *1 teaspoon cumin seeds*
> *½ teaspoon turmeric powder*
> *1 teaspoon coriander powder*
> *handful of coriander leaves*
> *salt to taste*

Wash *dal* 3 times. Soak in 8 cups water for 1 hour. In saucepan, cook in same water with turmeric till *dal* starts breaking down. Add salt and coriander leaves. Cook 5 minutes. Set aside. In frying pan, heat ghee. Add cumin seeds, bay leaves, and ginger. When color changes, add to *dal* with coriander powder. Mix well. Return to flame and cook 3–5 minutes on low. If *dal* is pasty, add more water. Serves 6–7.

Toora Dal

> *2 cups toora dal*
> *¼ cup peanuts, ground*
> *¼ cup grated coconut*

2 green chilis, finely chopped
3 tablespoons ghee
1 teaspoon garam masala
1 teaspoon mustard seeds
½ teaspoon turmeric powder
pinch of asafetida
salt to taste

Wash *dal* 3 times. Soak in 12 cups water for 2–3 hours. In saucepan, cook in same water with turmeric till *dal* starts breaking down. Remove from flame. In frying pan, heat ghee. Add mustard seeds and asafetida. When popping stops, add chilis, coconut, and peanuts, and fry briefly. Then add to *dal* with *garam masala*. Mix well, and cook 3–5 minutes on low flame. Serves 8–9.

Spicy Toora Dal

2 cups toora dal
1 big tomato, blanched and sliced
¼ cup grated coconut
2 green chilis, finely chopped
1-inch piece ginger root, grated
3 tablespoons ghee
1 tablespoon coriander seeds
1 teaspoon mustard seeds
½ teaspoon turmeric powder
1 teaspoon cumin powder
handful of coriander leaves
salt to taste

Wash *dal* 3 times. In saucepan, bring 12 cups water to boil. Add *dal* and turmeric. Cook till *dal* starts breaking down. Add tomatoes, chilis, coconut, and salt. Cook on low flame. In frying pan, heat ghee. Add coriander seeds and mustard seeds. When popping stops, add ginger. Fry briefly. Add to *dal* with cumin powder. Mix well, and cook 3–5 minutes. Garnish with coriander leaves. Serves 8–9.

Toora Dal & Pumpkin

2 cups toora dal
2 cups pumpkin, peeled and sliced
2 medium tomatoes, chopped small
¼ cup grated coconut
2 green chilis, finely chopped
3 tablespoons ghee
¼ teaspoon cumin seeds
¼ teaspoon mustard seeds
pinch of asafetida
½ teaspoon turmeric powder
1 teaspoon fenugreek seeds
handful of coriander leaves
salt to taste

Wash *dal* 3 times. Soak in water for a few hours. Drain. In frying pan, dry-roast fenugreek seeds till reddish. Grind into powder. In saucepan, heat ghee. Add cumin seeds, mustard seeds, and asafetida. When popping stops, add chilis, fenugreek powder, and tomatoes. Cook till soft. Add pumpkin, salt, and coconut. Fry for 5 minutes. Add *dal,* turmeric powder, and 12 cups water. Add salt to taste. Cook till *dal* breaks down. Garnish with coriander leaves. Serves 8–9.

Toora Dal & Sweet Potatoes

1 cup toora dal
2 cups sweet potatoes, peeled and sliced

1 green chili, finely chopped
1-inch piece ginger root, grated
3 tablespoons ghee
1 teaspoon cumin seeds
½ teaspoon turmeric powder
pinch of asafetida
handful of coriander leaves
salt to taste

Wash *dal* 3 times. Soak in 6 cups water for 1 hour. Cook in same water with turmeric powder and sweet potatoes till *dal* starts breaking down. Remove and mash into paste. In frying pan, heat ghee and add cumin seeds and asafetida. When color changes, add chilis and ginger and fry briefly. Mix in coriander leaves. Pour on *dal,* mix well. Serves 6–7.

Toora Dal & Tomatoes

2 cups toora dal
2 cups tomatoes, diced
1 green chili, finely chopped
1-inch piece ginger root, grated
1 tablespoon ghee
1 teaspoon cumin seeds
pinch of asafetida
½ teaspoon turmeric powder
½ teaspoon cinnamon powder
½ teaspoon cumin powder
handful of coriander leaves
salt to taste

Wash *dal* 3 times. Soak in 12 cups water for 1–2 hours. Cook in same water with turmeric and salt till *dal* starts breaking up. Add tomato, chili, and ginger. Cook 5 minutes. Add all powdered spices and mix well. When completely broken down, remove. In frying pan, heat ghee and add cumin seeds and asafetida. When color changes, add to *dal*. If *dal* is thick, add more water. Mix well. Cook 3–5 minutes. Serves 8–9.

Fancy Toora Dal

2 cups toora dal
½ cup urad dal
1 cup sweet potatoes, diced
¼ cup peanuts, pounded
2 green chilis, finely chopped
1-inch piece ginger root, grated
3 tablespoons ghee
1 teaspoon cumin seeds
½ teaspoon mustard seeds
pinch of asafetida
1 teaspoon garam masala
handful of coriander leaves
salt to taste

Wash *urad dal* 3 times. Soak overnight in enough water to cover 1 inch. Drain and grind into paste. Wash *toora dal* 3 times. Soak in 8 cups water for 1–2 hours. Cook in same water till broken down. Mash and put through sieve. Mix in sweet potatoes and peanuts. Mix well. Add 2 cups water and cook on low flame till potatoes are soft. Add 1 cup water. Continue cooking on low flame. In saucepan, heat ghee, and add cumin seeds, mustard seeds, and asafetida. When popping stops, add chili and ginger and fry briefly. Add *urad dal* paste. Fry till color changes. Mixing well, add *garam masala* and coriander leaves. Add to *toora dal* with 1 cup water. Cook 3–5 minutes on low flame or till thick. Serves 7–8.

Urad Dal

1½ cups urad dal, split
1 cup mixed vegetables, diced
1 green chili, finely chopped
1-inch piece ginger root, grated
½ teaspoon turmeric powder
3 tablespoons ghee
2 teaspoons anise or fennel seeds,
*   powdered*
handful of coriander leaves
salt to taste

Wash *dal* 3 times. Soak in 8 cups water for 1–2 hours. In saucepan, heat ghee. Add chili, ginger, and anise powder and fry briefly. Add vegetables, salt, and turmeric. Fry 2–3 minutes. Add *dal* and water. Cook on medium flame till *dal* breaks down. Garnish with coriander leaves. Serves 6–7.

Channa Dal

1 cup channa dal
½ cup peanuts, ground
1 teaspoon chickpea flour
2 tablespoons ghee
1 green chili, finely chopped
½ teaspoon turmeric powder
1 teaspoon garam masala
pinch of asafetida
handful of coriander leaves
salt to taste

Wash *dal* 3 times. Soak in 8 cups water overnight. Cook in same water with turmeric till *dal* becomes soft. If too thick, add more water. Add peanuts and salt. Mix well and continue cooking on low flame. In frying pan, heat ghee. Add chili, chickpea flour, and asafetida and mix well. Fry till flour turns reddish. Add to *dal* with *garam masala* and mix well. Cook 2–3 minutes. Garnish with coriander leaves. Serves 6–7.

Channa Dal & Coconut

1 cup channa dal
½ cup grated coconut
4 tablespoons ghee
1 green chili, finely chopped
1 teaspoon cumin seeds
1 teaspoon mustard seeds
½ teaspoon turmeric powder
pinch of asafetida
a few curry leaves
handful of coriander leaves
salt to taste

Wash *dal* 3 times. Soak in 4 cups water overnight. Drain and grind into paste. In saucepan, heat ghee. Add cumin seeds, mustard seeds, and asafetida. When popping stops, add chili and coconut. When color changes, add rest of ingredients with 2 cups water. Cook till dry, stirring occasionally. Serves 5–6.

Channa Dal & Tomatoes

1½ cups channa dal
1 cup tomato, finely chopped

1 green chili, finely chopped
½-inch piece ginger root, grated
3 tablespoons ghee
½ teaspoon cumin powder
½ teaspoon turmeric powder
1 teaspoon garam masala
1 teaspoon coriander powder
1 teaspoon cumin seeds
2 pinches asafetida
4 bay leaves
salt to taste

Wash *dal* 3 times. Soak in 10 cups water overnight. Cook in same water with turmeric till *dal* becomes soft. Add tomatoes, and salt. Cook 3–5 minutes. Add all powdered spices. Mix well. Continue cooking on low flame. In frying pan, heat ghee. Add cumin seeds, bay leaves, and asafetida. When color changes, add chili and ginger and fry briefly. Add to *dal*. Cook 1–2 minutes. Garnish with *garam masala*. Serves 7–8.

Split Pea Soup (Yellow or Green)

1 cup dried split peas
1 medium tomato, sliced
¼ cup grated coconut
2 green chilis, finely chopped
½-inch piece ginger root, grated
3 tablespoons ghee
1 teaspoon mustard seeds
½ teaspoon turmeric powder
pinch of asafetida

1 teaspoon coriander powder
1 teaspoon cumin powder
1 teaspoon garam masala
juice of 1 lime
salt to taste

Wash peas 3 times. Soak in 8 cups water for 1–2 hours. Cook in same water with turmeric till peas start to break down. Add coconut, tomato, and salt and mix well. Cook till completely broken down. Set aside. In frying pan, heat ghee. Add mustard seeds and asafetida. When popping stops, add chili and ginger and fry briefly. Add to *dal* with all remaining ingredients and 1 cup water. Cook 2–3 minutes. Serves 6–7.

Rice

Pepper Rice

1 cup rice
2 tablespoons ghee
1 teaspoon salt
1 teaspoon black pepper powder
2 pinches asafetida
handful of coriander leaves

In saucepan, bring 2 cups water and salt to boil. Add rice. Lower heat to simmer and cover tightly. Cook 20 minutes, or till soft. In frying pan, heat ghee. Add asafetida. When color changes, add pepper. Pour over rice. Mix well. Garnish with coriander leaves. Serves 3–4.

Tamarind Rice

1½ cups rice
20 cashews
1 tablespoon channa dal
1 tablespoon urad dal
3-inch ball of tamarind
*   or 2 tablespoons paste*
2 tablespoons ghee
1 tablespoon mustard seeds
1 teaspoon fenugreek, crushed
¼ teaspoon asafetida
1 teaspoon black pepper

1 teaspoon cumin powder
½ teaspoon turmeric powder
1 teaspoon salt

Cover tamarind with 2 cups warm water for 5 minutes. Squeeze out juice and set aside. (If using paste, mix with ½ cup water.) In saucepan, bring 3 cups water to a boil. Add rice, salt, and turmeric. Stir once to prevent sticking. Cover. Lower heat to simmer and cook 20 minutes. Set aside. Deep fry *urad dal, channa dal,* and cashews separately in ghee. Drain and mix into rice. Heat ghee. Add mustard seeds, fenugreek seeds, and asafetida. When popping stops, add tamarind water and all other spices. Fry briefly. Pour into rice. Mix well. Serves 4–5.

Rice & Curd (Yogurt)

1½ cups rice
1 tablespoon butter or ghee
3 cups yogurt
1½ teaspoons salt
2 tablespoons ghee
2 green chilis, finely chopped
1-inch piece ginger root, grated
1 teaspoon mustard seeds

In saucepan, bring 3 cups water to boil. Add rice. Stir once and cover. Lower heat to simmer and cook 20 minutes till rice is soft and separate. Mix in butter with yogurt, salt, chilis, and ginger. In frying pan, heat ghee. Add mustard seeds. When popping stops, add to rice and mix well. Serve 4–5.

Coconut Rice #1

1½ cups rice

4 teaspoons urad dal
4 tablespoons ghee
1 tablespoon channa dal
1 teaspoon chili powder
1 teaspoon salt
1 teaspoon mustard seeds
4 teaspoons urad dal, split
pinch of asafetida
2 cups grated coconut

In saucepan, bring 3 cups water to boil. Add rice and salt. Stir once and cover. Lower heat to simmer. Cook 20 minutes till soft and separate. Heat 2 tablespoons ghee. Add *channa dal* and 3 teaspoons *urad dal.* Fry till reddish in color. Add chili powder and fry briefly. Cool. Grind into paste and mix into rice. Heat remaining ghee. Add 1 teaspoon *urad dal,* mustard seeds, and asafetida. When popping stops, add rest of ingredients, including coconut. Turn down heat and fry till coconut changes color. Add to rice. Mix well. Serves 4–5.

Coconut Rice #2

1½ cups rice
2 cups grated coconut
a few strands of saffron
2 tablespoons turbinado sugar
5 tablespoons ghee
1 teaspoon cardamon powder
¼ cup pistachios
¼ cup cashews
¼ cup raisins
ghee for deep frying

Soak rice in water for 2 hours. Drain and dry for 1 hour. Deep-fry nuts till light brown. Slice. In frying pan, heat 3 tablespoons ghee. Add coconut and fry till reddish in color. Remove from heat. Soak saffron in 1 teaspoon warm water; mash into paste. In saucepan, heat remaining ghee. Add rice and fry briefly. Add 3 cups water and bring to boil. Stir once to prevent sticking. Lower heat to simmer, then cover. When rice is half done (about 10 minutes), add all other ingredients. Mix once. Cover and simmer till rice is tender and soft (about another 10 minutes). Serves 4–5.

Lemon Rice

1½ cups rice
2 tablespoons ghee
2 green chilis, finely chopped
1-inch piece ginger root, grated
1 teaspoon salt
1 teaspoon turmeric powder
3 tablespoons channa dal
1½ teaspoons mustard seeds
½ cup lemon juice
handful of coriander leaves

In saucepan, bring 3 cups water to boil. Add rice, salt, and turmeric. Stir once. Cover and lower heat to simmer. Cook 20 minutes till rice is soft and separate. Mix lemon juice, ginger, and chilis. Add to rice and mix well. Heat ghee. Add mustard seeds and *dal*. Fry till *dal* turns reddish in color. Pour into rice and mix well. Garnish with coriander leaves. Serves 4–5.

Saffron Rice

1½ cups rice

½ cup turbinado sugar
¼ cup sliced cashews, deep-fried
3 tablespoons ghee
¼ cup raisins
1 teaspoon cardamon powder
3 pinches saffron, soaked in
1 teaspoon warm water

Bring to boil 3 cups water. Add rice. Stir once. Cover. Lower heat to simmer. Cook rice till soft and separated. Mix sugar with ¼ cup water. Bring to boil. When sugar is dissolved, pour into rice, mixing well. Add fried cashews to cardamon and soaked saffron. (Saffron is better if ground into paste.) Mix well.

Rice & Eggplant

1½ cups rice
3 tablespoons ghee
1½ teaspoon mustard seeds
2 cups diced eggplant
juice of 3 limes
½ cup peas, shelled or frozen
2 green chilis, finely chopped
1 teaspoon salt
1 teaspoon turmeric powder

In saucepan, bring 3 cups water to a boil. Add rice, salt, and turmeric. Stir once. Cover and lower heat to simmer. Cook 20 minutes till soft and separated. In frying pan, heat ghee. Add mustard seeds. When popping stops, add chilis and vegetables along with ¼ cup of water. Stir, cover, and cook for 10 minutes. When vegetables are soft, add to rice. Mix well. Cook 5 minutes. Add lime juice. Mix and remove from flame. Serves 5–6.

Dal Pullao

1½ cups rice
5 tablespoons ghee
1½ cups yellow mung dal
½ pound baby potatoes, cut in half
1-inch piece ginger root, grated
1 teaspoon cumin seeds
4 cloves
½ teaspoon turbinado sugar
1-inch piece of cinnamon, broken into bits
3 bay leaves, crumbled
1 teaspoon turmeric
pinch of asafetida
handful of coriander leaves
1 teaspoon salt

Soak *dal* and rice separately for 2 hours. Drain. In saucepan, cook *dal* with 6 cups water till half done. Drain. In saucepan, heat 4 tablespoons ghee. Add asafetida, cinnamon, bay leaves, cloves, and ginger and fry briefly. Add turmeric, potatoes, and salt. Fry for 5 minutes. Add 1 cup water. Cover and cook till potatoes are half done. Mix in rice and *dal*. Add enough water to cover 1 inch. Bring to boil. Reduce heat. Cover and simmer. Cook 20 minutes till rice is tender and dry. Heat 1 tablespoon ghee. Add cumin seeds. When brown, add to rice. Garnish with coriander leaves. Serves 5–6.

Fancy Vegetable Rice

2 cups rice
3 cups mixed vegetables (potatoes, carrots, peas,
    cauliflower, beans, etc.), peeled and sliced

3 large tomatoes, blanched and sliced
7 tablespoons ghee
2 green chilis, finely chopped
1-inch piece ginger root, grated
1 teaspoon turmeric powder
bay leaves, crushed
¼ teaspoon cardamon powder
4 cloves
½-inch cinnamon stick
1 teaspoon black cumin (optional)
¼ cup cashews
¼ cup pistachios
¼ cup raisins
a few strands of saffron
1 teaspoon turbinado sugar
pinch of asafetida
1 teaspoon sesame seeds
2 tablespoons grated coconut
a few curry leaves
handful of coriander leaves
salt to taste
ghee for deep frying

Wash and soak rice for 1 hour. Drain and dry for 1 hour. Deep-fry nuts till light brown. Slice. In saucepan, heat 4 tablespoons ghee. Add all whole spices and fry briefly. Add chilis and ginger. Fry till brown, then add vegetables. Fry for 5 minutes. Add tomatoes, salt, sugar, and turmeric powder. Fry till tomatoes are soft. Add 1 cup water, cover, and cook on low flame till vegetables are half done. Add rice and rest of ingredients and mix well. Add enough water to cover 1 inch. Bring to boil. Cover and lower heat to simmer. Cook 20 minutes till rice is tender and soft. In frying pan, heat 3 tablespoons ghee. When smoking, pour over rice. Garnish with coriander leaves. Serves 7–8.

Potato Rice

2 cups rice
1 cup yellow mung dal
2 cups potatoes, sliced
¼ cup ghee
2 green chilis, finely chopped
½-inch piece ginger root, grated
1 cup green peas, shelled
2 bay leaves, crumbled
1 small piece of coconut, sliced
2 tablespoons yogurt
1 teaspoon turbinado sugar
1 teaspoon cumin seeds
2 pinches asafetida
1 teaspoon cardamon powder
4 cloves
1-inch piece of cinnamon stick
½ teaspoon coriander powder
handful of coriander leaves
salt to taste

Wash and soak *dal* and rice separately for 1 hour. Drain. Grind into paste ginger, chilis, coconut, and coriander leaves. Mix in yogurt, sugar, salt, and turmeric. In saucepan, cook *dal* in 6 cups water till soft. Drain. In saucepan, heat ghee. Add whole spices. Cook till color changes. Add paste and mix well. Cook for 1 minute. Mix in rice and *dal* and fry for 5 minutes. Add enough water to cover 1 inch. Stir once so rice doesn't stick. Bring to boil. Cover and lower heat to simmer, cooking 20 minutes till rice is tender and soft. Garnish with coriander leaves. Serves 8–9.

Masala Pullao

2 cups rice
4 tablespoons ghee
3 big tomatoes, blanched and chopped
2 cups peas, shelled
2 green chilis, finely chopped
1-inch piece of cinnamon stick
4 cloves
2 bay leaves
pinch of asafetida
½ teaspoon mustard seeds
1 teaspoon turmeric powder
2 tablespoons grated coconut
handful of coriander leaves
1 teaspoon salt

Soak rice in 4 cups water with salt for a few hours. In saucepan, heat ghee. Add mustard seeds, cumin seeds, and asafetida and mix well. When popping stops, add turmeric, chilis, bay leaves, cloves, and cinnamon. Fry briefly. Add tomato. Stir. Add rice and water. Bring to boil. Stir well once to prevent sticking. Bring to boil. Reduce heat to simmer, cover, and cook 20 minutes till rice is soft and separated. Garnish with coriander leaves. Serves 6–7.

Curd Pullao

2 cups rice
curd made from ½ gallon milk
ghee for deep frying
¼ cup sliced almonds
¼ cup raisins

¼ cup cashews
½ cup grated coconut
½ teaspoon chili powder
¼ teaspoon cardamon powder
5 tablespoons ghee
4 cloves
2 bay leaves
½ teaspoon cinnamon powder
a few peppercorns
1 teaspoon coriander seeds
1-inch piece ginger root, grated
handful of coriander leaves
1 teaspoon salt

Tie ginger, peppercorns, cloves, and coriander seeds in muslin cloth. In saucepan, put 4 cups water and boil down to 2 cups. Squeeze out muslin cloth and discard. Cut curd into 1-inch pieces and deep-fry in ghee till light brown. Drain. Heat 2 tablespoons ghee. Add nuts, raisins, and coconut. Fry on low heat till coconut becomes reddish in color. Remove and set aside. Soak rice in water for 1 hour; drain and set aside. Soak saffron in 1 teaspoon warm milk for 5 minutes, then grind into paste. Set aside. Heat 5 tablespoons ghee. Add bay leaves. When light brown, add rice, salt, and sugar and mix well. Fry on low flame for 5 minutes. Add spiced water plus 2 cups extra water. Stir well. Bring to boil. Cover and simmer for 20 minutes. When done, add all other ingredients and mix well. Cook covered till rice is soft and separate (about 10 minutes). Garnish with coriander leaves. Serves 6–7.

Bean Pullao

2 cups rice
3 tablespoons ghee

1 cup sliced green beans (any kind)
1-inch stick of cinnamon
2 cloves
¼ teaspoon black pepper powder
¼ teaspoon cardamon powder
¼ cup dill weed, finely chopped
pinch of asafetida
1 teaspoon salt

In saucepan, cook beans in a little water with salt till soft. Drain and set aside. In saucepan, heat ghee. Add cinnamon, pepper, cloves, and asafetida and mix well. Fry briefly. Add rice and fry for 5 minutes on low flame, stirring constantly. Add 4 cups water. Stir and bring to boil. Reduce heat to simmer, cover, and cook 20 minutes. Mix in rest of ingredients. Serves 6–7.

Sweet Pullao

2 cups rice
¼ cup cashews
¼ cup almonds, sliced
¼ cup raisins
a few pistachios
1 tablespoon fresh curd
2 cups milk
1-inch piece ginger root, grated
½ cup turbinado sugar
a few drops rose water
5 tablespoons ghee
2 cardamon pods
4 cloves
1-inch piece of cinnamon stick
½ teaspoon black cumin

1 teaspoon channa dal
1 teaspoon cumin seeds
a few peppercorns
4 bay leaves

Wash rice and dry in sun for 2 hours on a window sill. In saucepan, cook down milk to ¼ cup, stirring constantly. Set aside. Tie ginger, black cumin, *dal,* cumin seeds, and peppercorns in muslin cloth. Boil in 8 cups water till reduced to 4 cups. Squeeze and discard muslin cloth. Pound cardamon, cloves, and cinnamon to a coarse powder. In saucepan, heat ghee. Add bay leaves and rice. Fry on low flame for 5 minutes. Add all ingredients, along with spiced water. Mix well. Bring to boil. Reduce heat to simmer, cover, and cook 20 minutes till rice is soft and separate. Serves 6–7.

Pineapple Pullao

2 cups rice
3 cups pineapple slices
½ cup turbinado sugar
1 cup ghee
1 tablespoon garam masala
a few almonds
½ teaspoon saffron,
*   soaked in ½ cup warm milk*

In saucepan, cook pineapples with sugar and ½ cup water till thick and syrupy. Remove and set aside. Wash and drain rice. In saucepan, heat ghee. Add *garam masala* and fry briefly. Add rice. Cook on low flame 5 minutes, stirring constantly. Add 4 cups water. Bring to boil. Reduce heat to simmer, cover, and cook 20 minutes. Add all ingredients and mix well. Serves 8–9.

Vegetables

Fried Cabbage

1 medium cabbage, grated
3 tablespoons ghee
½ cup grated coconut
1 teaspoon urad dal
2 green chilis, finely chopped
½ teaspoon turmeric powder
1 teaspoon mustard seeds
handful of coriander leaves
salt to taste

In skillet, heat ghee. Add mustard seeds, *dal,* and chilis. Fry till *dal* turns red. Add turmeric and fry briefly. Add cabbage and salt. Cover tightly and cook on low flame without water till soft. Garnish with coriander leaves. Serves 7–8.

Cabbage & Potatoes

1 medium cabbage, grated
4 medium potatoes, peeled and diced
3 large tomatoes, blanched and sliced
2 green chilis, finely chopped
4 tablespoons ghee
1-inch piece ginger root, grated

1 teaspoon turmeric powder
3 bay leaves
2 teaspoons garam masala
salt to taste

Heat ghee. Add bay leaves, potatoes, and cabbage, and fry till light brown, stirring constantly. Add all other ingredients except *garam masala* and mix well. Fry briefly. Add 1 cup water. Cover and cook on low flame for 5 minutes. Either garnish with *garam masala* or mix it in. Serves 8–9.

Cabbage & Coconut Loaf

1 large cabbage, grated
2 cups grated coconut
4 tablespoons ghee
2 green chilis, finely chopped
1 teaspoon cumin,
    dry-roasted and powdered
½ teaspoon turmeric powder
1 teaspoon garam masala
¼ teaspoon asafetida
½ teaspoon baking soda
handful of coriander leaves
salt to taste

Preheat oven to 350°F or 177°C. In mixing bowl, stir all ingredients together into a nice batter. In frying pan, heat ghee. When hot, add to mixture. Place mixture in greased baking pan and bake 20–25 minutes. Serves 8–9.

Cabbage & Peas

1 cup grated cabbage
1 cup green peas, shelled and boiled
3 tablespoons ghee
1 green chili, finely chopped
1-inch piece ginger root, grated
1 teaspoon mustard seeds
½ teaspoon turmeric powder
1 teaspoon mango powder
2 pinches asafetida
a few neem leaves
salt to taste

In skillet, heat ghee. Add mustard seeds, asafetida, and neem leaves. When popping stops, add chili and ginger and fry briefly. Add cabbage, peas, turmeric, and salt and mix well. Cover and cook on low flame till cabbage is soft. Add mango powder. Mix well. Serves 3–4.

Cabbage & Dal

1 medium cabbage, thinly sliced
½ cup yellow or green mung dal, split
½ cup grated coconut
2 tablespoons ghee
1 green chili, finely chopped
1 teaspoon ground cumin seeds
½ teaspoon mustard seeds
⅛ teaspoon asafetida
juice of 1 lime
salt to taste

Soak *dal* overnight. Next day, drain out water. In skillet, heat ghee. Add mustard seeds and asafetida. When seeds stop popping, add *dal*. Cook for 2–3 minutes. Add cabbage, coconut, 1 cup water, and cumin. Mix well. Cover and cook on low flame till *dal* is soft. Add lime juice and garnish with chopped coriander leaves. Serves 5–6.

Cabbage & Cucumbers

1 medium cabbage, finely sliced
3 cucumbers, peeled and sliced small
1 green chili, finely chopped
juice of 1 lime
4 tablespoons ghee
1½ teaspoon mustard seeds
1 teaspoon turmeric powder
a few neem leaves
salt to taste

In skillet, heat ghee. Add mustard seeds. When popping stops, add chilis and neem leaves and fry briefly. Add cabbage, turmeric, and salt. Cover and cook on low flame without water till soft. Add lime juice and cucumbers. Mix well. Cook 1–2 more minutes. Serves 6–7.

Cabbage Slices

1 medium cabbage, grated
1 cup chickpea flour
1 cup whole wheat flour
2 green chilis, finely chopped
¼ cup grated coconut
3 tablespoons ghee
1 tablespoon sesame seeds

1 teaspoon turmeric powder
1 teaspoon mustard seeds
¼ teaspoon asafetida
1 teaspoon garam masala
1-inch piece ginger root, grated
handful of coriander leaves
salt to taste

Dry-roast sesame seeds and ⅛ cup coconut. Set aside. Grind into paste green chilis, ginger, and coriander leaves. Mix all ingredients together except mustard seeds, asafetida, and remaining coconut, and make a soft dough. If necessary, add a little water. Roll dough into long, thin rolls and steam for ½ hour. Slice into thin slices and set aside. Heat ghee. Add mustard seeds and asafetida. When popping stops, add slices of cabbage and fry on low flame till lightly brown. Garnish with remaining coconut. Serves 6–7.

Cabbage Rolls

1 large cabbage
2 medium potatoes,
    peeled and diced
½ cup shelled peas, boiled
1 carrot, diced
1-inch piece ginger root, grated
7 tablespoons ghee
1 green chili
¼ teaspoon asafetida
1 teaspoon anise seed,
    dry-roasted and powdered
juice of 1 lime
1 teaspoon salt

Separate leaves from cabbage, putting large ones aside. Grate remaining cabbage. In skillet, grind into paste ginger, chili, and anise
seed powder. Heat 3 tablespoons ghee. Add turmeric, asafetida,
and salt and fry briefly. Add potatoes and carrot. Cover and cook
without water till vegetables are tender (if required, add a small
amount of water.) Mix in peas and all other ingredients. Cook 5
minutes. Make into paste. Open each cabbage leaf and spread
paste evenly. Roll and tie with string. Heat 4 tablespoons ghee
in wide frying pan. Add rolls. Cover and cook on low flame for
5 minutes. Turn and fry till light brown on both sides. Serves
8–9.

Cabbage (Fancy Style)

1 medium cabbage, shredded
1 green chili
1-inch piece ginger root
½ cup peanuts, roasted and ground
½ cup raisins
3 tablespoons ghee
1 teaspoon coriander powder
1 teaspoon cumin powder
½ teaspoon turmeric powder
½ teaspoon mustard seeds
juice of 1 lime
handful of coriander leaves
salt to taste

Grind ginger and chili into paste. In skillet, heat ghee. Add mustard seeds. When popping stops, add all spices, raisins, and peanuts. Fry briefly. Add cabbage. Cover tightly and cook without
water on low flame till cabbage is soft. Garnish with coriander
leaves and lime juice. Serves 6–7.

Cabbage & Pineapple

1 medium cabbage, chopped
2 cups diced pineapples (without juice)
1 green chili, finely chopped
1-inch piece ginger root, grated
3 tablespoons ghee
1 teaspoon cumin seeds
½ teaspoon cinnamon powder
½ teaspoon turmeric powder
1 teaspoon garam masala
1 teaspoon coriander powder
handful of coriander leaves
salt to taste

Deep-fry pineapple till brown (add to hot ghee slowly and carefully, as the ghee may spatter.) Drain and set aside. In skillet, heat ghee. Add cumin seeds, chilis, and ginger. When light brown, add cabbage, turmeric, and salt. Mix well, cover, and cook on low flame till soft. Add coriander, cinnamon, and *garam masala*. Mix well. Add pineapple and cook 1–2 minutes. Garnish with coriander leaves. Serves 7–8.

Cauliflower & Yogurt

3 cups grated cauliflower
1 cup yogurt
1 green chili, finely chopped
2 tablespoons ghee
1 teaspoon cumin seeds
pinch of asafetida
handful of coriander leaves
salt to taste

In skillet, heat ghee. Add cumin, asafetida, and chilis. Fry till color changes, then add cauliflower and fry briefly. Add yogurt and salt. Cover and cook till thick. Garnish with coriander leaves. Serves 4–5.

South Indian Cauliflower

1 medium cauliflower,
  broken into flowerets
1 cup grated coconut
1 green chili, finely chopped
1 teaspoon urad dal
2 tablespoons ghee
1 teaspoon cumin seeds
½ teaspoon mustard seeds
½ teaspoon turmeric powder
salt to taste

Grind chilis, cumin seeds, and coconut into paste with a little water. In saucepan, put 2 cups water. Add cauliflower, salt, and turmeric. Mix well. Cover and cook till tender but firm. Heat ghee. Add mustard seeds and *dal*. When popping stops and *dal* is reddish in color, add cauliflower and paste. Mix well. Cook 1–2 minutes. Serves 5–6.

North Indian Cauliflower

1 large cauliflower, broken into flowerets
2 green chilis, finely chopped
1-inch piece ginger root, grated
3 tablespoons ghee
1 teaspoon cumin seeds

1 teaspoon anise seeds
½ teaspoon fenugreek
½ teaspoon turmeric powder
1 teaspoon coriander powder
⅛ teaspoon asafetida
handful of coriander leaves
salt to taste

In skillet, heat ghee. Add asafetida, cumin, fenugreek, and anise seeds. Cook briefly. Add ginger and chilis. When brown, add cauliflower, turmeric, and salt and fry briefly. Add 1 cup water. Cover and cook on low flame till cauliflower is soft. More water can be added, but only ½ cup at a time. Serves 6–7.

Cauliflower, Potatoes, & Peas

1 large cauliflower, cut into flowerets
3 medium potatoes, peeled and diced
1 cup peas
½ cup sour yogurt
1 green chili, finely chopped
3 tablespoons ghee
1 teaspoon cumin powder
½ teaspoon turmeric powder
3 bay leaves
1 teaspoon garam masala
1 teaspoon coriander powder
salt to taste

Deep-fry cauliflower till brown; drain and set aside. In saucepan, boil peas till soft; drain. In skillet, heat ghee. Add potatoes. Cook briefly, then add cumin, turmeric, bay leaves, chili, and coriander. Mix well. Cover and cook on low flame without water, stirring occasionally. When potatoes are soft, add peas, cauliflower, and salt. Mix well. Beat 1 cup water with yogurt and add to mixture, mixing well. Cover and cook on low flame for a few minutes. Add *garam masala*. Remove from flame. Serves 8–9.

Cauliflower with Green Peas

1 large cauliflower
2 cups peas
1 green chili, finely chopped
2 tablespoons ghee
1 teaspoon cumin seeds
½ teaspoon turmeric powder
¼ teaspoon asafetida
handful of coriander leaves
salt to taste

Chop cauliflower into small pieces. Wash, and steam them in a little water for 2 minutes, then drain. In separate pot, boil peas till soft. Set aside. In skillet, heat ghee. Add cumin seeds, chilis, and asafetida. Cook till color changes, then add cauliflower, peas, turmeric, and salt. Cook on low flame till tender. Garnish with coriander leaves. Serves 5–6.

Steamed Cauliflower & Coconut

1 large cauliflower
1 green chili, finely chopped
½ cup grated coconut
juice of 1 lime
1 teaspoon cumin powder
salt to taste

Cut cauliflower into small pieces. In saucepan, steam in a little water till tender but firm. Drain out water and mix in other ingredients. This is a very healthful and tasty preparation. Serves 6–7.

Cauliflower & Tomatoes With Fried Paneer

1 large cauliflower
6 large tomatoes
4 cups milk
1 green chili, finely chopped
3 tablespoons ghee
ghee for deep frying
1-inch piece ginger root,
*   finely chopped*
¼ teaspoon asafetida
½ teaspoon turmeric powder
handful of coriander leaves

In saucepan, boil milk and turn to curd with lemon juice. Put in muslin cloth and press with heavy weight for 1 hour. Cut cauliflower into flowerets about 1 inch long. Wash and steam them in a little water till tender but firm. Boil tomatoes in water till skin cracks. Drain off water and mash to pulp. Extract juice by putting through a fine sieve. Set aside. In skillet, heat ghee. Add asafetida and ginger and cook till color changes, then add tomato and salt. Cook for 5 minutes. Add cauliflower. Let cook on low flame. Cut curd into 1-inch squares. Deep-fry in ghee till brown; drain, and add to cauliflower. When curd becomes soft, remove from heat. Garnish with coriander leaves. Serves 6–7.

Spiced Cauliflower

1 large cauliflower
ghee for deep frying
2 tablespoons ghee
2 green chilis, finely chopped
2 cloves
½ tablespoon black pepper powder
2-inch piece of cinnamon stick
1 teaspoon cumin seeds
2 bay leaves
¼ teaspoon asafetida
2 teaspoons coriander powder
½ teaspoon turmeric powder
1 teaspoon poppy seeds
½ cup raisins
handful of coriander leaves
salt to taste

Cut cauliflower into 1-inch flowerets and deep-fry in ghee till light brown. Drain and set aside. In saucepan, put 2 cups water. Tie muslin cloth around pepper, cloves, cinnamon, and poppy seeds and add to water. Boil till 1 cup of water remains and remove cloth. Set aside. In skillet, heat ghee and add cumin seeds, bay leaves, asafetida, and chilis. Fry till color changes, then add spiced water, cauliflower, and all other ingredients. Cook for 3–5 minutes. Garnish with coriander leaves. Serves 5–6.

Fancy Cauliflower

1 large cauliflower,
   broken into flowerets
¼ cup grated coconut

3 tablespoons ghee
1 green chili, finely chopped
1-inch piece ginger root, grated
2 cloves
½ stick cinnamon
2 pinches cardamon powder, or 4 pods
1 teaspoon mustard seeds
½ teaspoon turmeric powder
⅛ teaspoon asafetida
handful of coriander leaves
salt to taste

In frying pan, dry-roast cloves, cinnamon, and coconut. When reddish in color, grind into paste with a little water. In skillet, heat ghee. Add cumin seeds, mustard seeds, and asafetida. When popping stops, add ginger and chilis and fry briefly. Add turmeric, salt, and cauliflower. Mix well. Cover and cook without water on low flame. When soft, add paste and 1 cup water. Mix well. Add cardamon. Cook till gravy is thick. Garnish with coriander leaves. Serves 5–6.

Cauliflower & Potatoes With Fried Paneer

2 medium cauliflowers,
*   broken up into flowerets*
6 large potatoes, cut same
*   size as flowerets*
4 cups milk
ghee for deep frying
2 tablespoons ghee
2 green chilis, finely chopped
1-inch piece ginger root, grated
1 teaspoon cumin seeds

1 teaspoon mustard seeds
½ teaspoon cinnamon powder
2 bay leaves
¼ teaspoon asafetida
½ teaspoon turmeric powder
1 teaspoon cumin powder
1 teaspoon garam masala
½ teaspoon cardamon powder
handful of coriander leaves
salt to taste

In saucepan, boil milk and turn into curd with lemon juice. Put in muslin cloth and press with heavy weight for 1 hour. Deep-fry cauliflower in ghee till light brown, then drain. Deep-fry potatoes in ghee till light brown; drain. Cut curd into cubes (any size), then deep-fry in ghee till brown; drain. In saucepan, heat ghee. Add cumin seeds, mustard seeds, and asafetida. When popping stops, add bay leaves, chilis, and ginger and fry briefly. Add 6 cups water and bring to boil. Add coriander powder, cumin powder, turmeric, and salt. Lower heat and boil for 5 minutes. Add cauliflower, potatoes, and fried curd with remaining ingredients. Cook 5–10 minutes, stirring occasionally. Garnish with coriander leaves. Serves 10–11.

Stuffed Korella

8 medium-sized korella
¼ cup chickpea flour
1 tablespoon cumin powder
1 tablespoon coriander powder
1 teaspoon turmeric powder
juice of 1 lime
6 tablespoons ghee
salt to taste

Slit each korella halfway through. Remove centers. Sprinkle with salt and set aside 4–5 hours. In mixing bowl, stir all other ingredients together. Stuff into korella. Tie string around korella so stuffing won't fall out. In large frying pan, heat ghee. Add korella. Cook on low flame, turning occasionally till soft and brownish in color. Remove strings. Serves 8.

Fancy Korella

2½ cups diced korella (remove seeds)
¼ cup sesame seeds,
*   roasted and pounded*
¼ cup peanuts, roasted and pounded
15 cashews, pounded
5 tablespoons ghee
¼ cup grated coconut
2 dried red chilis, broken
1 tablespoon turbinado sugar
1 teaspoon mustard seeds
1 teaspoon garam masala
¼ teaspoon black pepper powder
salt to taste

In skillet, heat 4 tablespoons ghee. Add korella. Cover and cook till browned. Add all ingredients except chilis and mustard seeds. Add ½ cup water and mix well. Cover and cook till a nice gravy has formed. Heat 1 tablespoon ghee. Add mustard seeds and chilis. When popping stops, add to korella mixture. Mix well and serve hot. Serves 4–5.

Korella & Channa Dal

2½ cups diced korella (remove seeds)

1 cup channa dal
5 tablespoons ghee
1 teaspoon mustard seeds
½ teaspoon turmeric powder
1 tablespoon cumin powder
⅛ teaspoon asafetida
handful of coriander leaves
salt to taste

Soak *dal* in 4 cups water overnight. The next day, drain and grind into paste. In skillet, heat ghee. Add mustard seeds and asafetida. When popping stops, add korella and fry till tender but firm. Add remaining ingredients except coriander leaves. Mix well. Cover and cook on low flame till done (about 15 minutes). Garnish with coriander leaves. Serves 4–5.

Korella & Coconut

2½ cups diced korella (remove seeds)
1 cup grated coconut
4 cloves
6 tablespoons ghee
2-inch piece of cinnamon
a few peppercorns
⅛ teaspoon asafetida
½ teaspoon mustard seeds
1 tablespoon turbinado sugar
¼ teaspoon red chili powder
handful of coriander leaves
salt to taste

In frying pan, heat 2 tablespoons ghee. Add cloves, cinnamon, coconut, peppercorns, and asafetida. When coconut turns reddish, remove and grind into paste. In skillet, heat 4 tablespoons ghee. Add mustard seeds. When popping stops, add korella. Fry till brown. Add rest of ingredients and mix well. Cover and cook on low flame for 2–3 minutes. Garnish with coriander leaves. Serves 4–5.

Corn & Yogurt

4 ears corn
1 cup yogurt beaten with 1 cup water
1 green chili, finely chopped
½-inch piece ginger root, grated
3 tablespoons ghee
½ teaspoon cumin seeds
1 teaspoon cumin powder
1 teaspoon coriander powder
½ teaspoon garam masala
½ teaspoon turmeric powder
handful of coriander leaves
salt to taste

Wash and grate corn. In saucepan, heat ghee. Add cumin seeds. When brown, add corn. Fry 3–5 minutes. Add all spices. Stir constantly for 2–3 minutes. Add yogurt. Cover and cook on low flame till thick. Garnish with coriander leaves. Serves 3–4.

Corn Shak

5 ears corn or 2 cups frozen corn
2 tablespoons grated coconut
3 tablespoons ghee
1 green chili, finely chopped
½-inch piece ginger root, grated

½ teaspoon mustard seeds
½ teaspoon turmeric powder
1 teaspoon cumin powder
1 teaspoon coriander powder
2 cloves
⅛ teaspoon asafetida
handful of coriander leaves
salt to taste

Wash and grate corn. In slillet, heat 2 tablespoons ghee. Add asa-fetida and fry till color changes, then add corn and fry 3–5 minutes. Add all ground spices. Fry 2–3 minutes. Cover and cook on low flame till almost dry. In frying pan, heat 1 tablespoon ghee. Add mustard seeds, ginger, and chili. When popping stops, pour in corn mixture, mix well, and garnish with coriander leaves. Serves 3–4.

Corn & Potatoes

5 ears fresh corn, or 2 cups frozen corn
2 medium potatoes, boiled,
   peeled, and mashed
½ cup dry-roasted peanuts, pounded
3 tablespoons ghee
1 green chili, finely chopped
1-inch piece ginger root, grated
2 tablespoons grated coconut
juice of 1 lime
1 teaspoon ground cumin
½ teaspoon turmeric powder
⅛ teaspoon asafetida
a few curry leaves
handful of coriander leaves
salt to taste

Wash and grate corn. In saucepan, put ½ cup water and stir in corn. Cook till tender. In skillet, heat ghee. Add asafetida, ginger, chilis, and curry leaves. When color changes, add rest of spices and fry briefly. Add corn and potatoes. Mix well and fry till light brown. Garnish with coriander leaves and lime juice. Serves 4–5.

Corn Curry

1 cup corn cut from the cob, boiled
2½ cups blanched tomatoes, slices
2 cups buttermilk
3 tablespoons ghee
1 green chili, finely chopped
1 teaspoon cumin seeds
1 teaspoon coriander seeds
¼ teaspoon black pepper
½ teaspoon turmeric powder
handful of coriander leaves
salt to taste

Grind all spices with chilis to paste. In skillet, heat ghee, then add corn and paste. Fry for 5 minutes. Add tomatoes and cook till soft. Add buttermilk. Cover and cook till thick. Garnish with coriander leaves. Serves 3–4.

Fried Eggplant

1 large eggplant
1 teaspoon coriander powder
½ teaspoon black pepper powder
½ teaspoon garam masala
½ teaspoon mango powder (amchur)

1 teaspoon cumin powder
¼ teaspoon chili powder
salt to taste
4 tablespoons ghee

Mix all spices together. Set aside. Slice eggplant into thin rounds. Carefully make slits in rounds and rub spices in well, especially in all the slits. In frying pan on medium flame, heat ghee and place in eggplants, slits down. Cook covered on low flame till light brown, turning occasionally. Repeat until all eggplant is done. Serves 3–4.

South Indian Stuffed Eggplant

8 Japanese eggplants
8 tablespoons ghee
1 teaspoon urad dal
½ cup grated coconut (optional garnish)
1 green chili pepper, finely chopped
½ teaspoon turmeric powder
1 teaspoon cumin seeds
5 peppercorns
1 teaspoon coriander seeds
½ teaspoon sesame seeds
handful of coriander leaves
salt to taste

In frying pan, heat 3 tablespoons ghee. Add all spices except salt and turmeric. When mixture becomes reddish in color, remove from flame. Add salt and turmeric. Grind into paste and set aside. Wash and cut eggplant. In 3- or 4-inch sections, slice in quarters half way through. Put 1 tablespoon of mixture in each section; set aside. In saucepan, heat 5 tablespoons ghee and put in stuffed eggplant. Cover and cook without water on low flame till soft. You may garnish with powdered coconut. Serves 7–8.

South Indian Eggplant Curry

> *3 medium eggplants,*
> *cut into small pieces*
> *4 tablespoons ghee*
> *2 green chilis, finely chopped*
> *1 teaspoon channa dal*
> *1 teaspoon sesame seeds*
> *⅛ teaspoon asafetida*
> *½ teaspoon turmeric powder*
> *½ teaspoon coconut powder*
> *1 teaspoon mustard seeds*
> *a few curry leaves*
> *a handful of coriander leaves*
> *salt to taste*

In frying pan, heat 2 tablespoons ghee. Add chilies, cumin seeds, coriander seeds, sesame seeds, and *dal*. When *dal* turns red, add coconut. Fry briefly, then grind into a paste. In skillet, heat 2 tablespoons ghee. Add mustard seeds and turmeric. When popping stops, add eggplant, salt, and curry leaves. Fry constantly. turning till eggplant changes color. Add paste of spices, and continue cooking for 3–5 minutes. Remove from flame and garnish with coconut and coriander leaves. Serves 6–8.

North Indian Eggplant #1

> *2 medium eggplants,*
> *cut into 2-inch cubes*

5 tablespoons ghee
½ cup grated coconut
1 tablespoon coriander seeds
a few peppercorns
4 cloves
⅛ teaspoon asafetida
½ teaspoon turmeric powder
handful of coriander leaves
salt to taste

In frying pan, heat 2 tablespoons ghee. Add coriander seeds, peppercorns, cloves, and asafetida. When spices become fragrant and light brown, add coconut. Fry briefly. Remove and grind into a paste; set aside. In saucepan, heat 3 tablespoons ghee. Add eggplant, turmeric, salt, and 1 cup water. Cover and cook on low flame till soft. Mix in paste well. Cover. Cook 1–3 minutes. Remove and garnish with coconut and coriander leaves. Serves 6–7.

North Indian Eggplant #2

3 large eggplants
2 tablespoons ghee
2 green chilis, finely chopped
¼ cup grated coconut
½ teaspoon ground black pepper
handful of coriander leaves
salt to taste

Place eggplant on open flame, turning till skin becomes black and wrinkled. Add cold water and peel off skin. Mash and set aside. In large frying pan, heat ghee, add chilis and cook till soft and light brown. Mix in rest of ingredients. Mix well. Remove from flame. Garnish with coriander leaves. Serves 6–7.

Spicy Eggplant

15 small eggplants
3 tablespoons ghee
1 cup sour yogurt
1 green chili, finely chopped
1 teaspoon cumin seeds
½ teaspoon mustard seeds
¼ teaspoon fenugreek seeds,
  crushed
½ teaspoon turmeric powder
handful of coriander leaves
salt to taste

Wash and dry eggplant. Cut into small pieces. In frying pan, dry-roast mustard seeds and cumin seeds. Grind into powder. Mix 1 cup water with yogurt and beat well. In skillet, heat ghee. Add fenugreek and green chilis and cook till light brown. Add eggplant and powdered spices. Fry till skins turn color and are soft. Add yogurt. Mix well. Cook till thick. Garnish with coriander leaves. Serves 6–8.

Eggplant & Spinach #1

2 medium eggplants
2 tablespoons ghee
4 cups spinach, chopped
salt to taste

Wash and cut eggplant into small pieces. In medium saucepan, heat ghee. Add eggplant and fry for 5 minutes, then add spinach, ½ cup water, and salt. Cover and cook on low flame till eggplant is soft. Serves 6–7.

Eggplant & Spinach #2

2 medium eggplants,
*   cut into 1-inch pieces*
3 tablespoons ghee
4 cups spinach, chopped
2 green chilis, finely chopped
1-inch piece ginger root, grated
½ teaspoon fenugreek seeds, crushed
1 teaspoon cumin seeds
1 teaspoon mustard seeds
1 teaspoon garam masala
½ teaspoon turmeric powder
handful of coriander or parsley leaves
salt to taste

In large saucepan, heat ghee. Add fenugreek, mustard, and cumin seeds. When popping stops, add chilis and ginger and fry briefly. Add eggplant, turmeric, and salt. Fry 5 minutes. Add spinach, ½ cup water, and all other ingredients. Mix well. Cover and cook over low flame till soft. Garnish with coriander or parsley leaves. Serves 6–7.

Eggplant & Tomatoes

2 medium eggplants
3 tablespoons ghee
4 large tomatoes, blanched and skinned
2 green chilis, finely chopped
¼ cup raisins
1 teaspoon mustard seeds
handful of coriander leaves
salt to taste

Wash and cut eggplants into 1-inch pieces. In large saucepan, heat ghee. Add mustard seeds. When popping stops, add eggplants, turmeric, ½ cup water, and salt and mix well. Cover and cook on low flame for 5–7 minutes. Add all other ingredients. Mix well, cover, and cook till soft. Garnish with coriander leaves. Serves 6–7.

Eggplant Salad

1 large eggplant
1 green chili, finely chopped
1-inch piece ginger root, grated
1 teaspoon cumin seeds,
    dry-roasted and powdered
juice of 1 lime or ½ lemon
2 tablespoons olive oil
salt to taste

Hold eggplant over gas flame or open flame, turning till skin turns black. Soak in cold water and peel. In medium saucepan, mash in all ingredients. Grated carrots, beets, cucumbers, and sliced tomatoes, can be added. Serves 5–6.

Eggplant Rounds

2 large eggplants, sliced in rounds
2 tablespoons ghee
2 tablespoons sesame seeds
1 teaspoon urad dal
1 teaspoon cumin seeds
¼ cup coconut
1 teaspoon garam masala
½ teaspoon chili powder

½ teaspoon turmeric powder
salt to taste

Deep-fry eggplant rounds till brown on each side. Drain and place on flat pan. In frying pan, heat ghee. Add cumin seeds and *dal*. When *dal* turns red, add sesame seeds and coconut and fry briefly. Grind into paste. Mix in all powdered spices and spread on eggplant rounds. Serves 6–8.

Stuffed Eggplant

10 Japanese eggplants,
*   cut 2–3 inches long*
6 tablespoons ghee
¼ cup grated coconut
1 green chili, finely chopped
1-inch piece ginger root, grated
1 teaspoon chickpea flour
1 teaspoon garam masala
1 tablespoon sesame seeds,
*   dry-roasted and powdered*
1 teaspoon coriander powder
½ teaspoon turmeric powder
1 teaspoon cumin powder
¼ cup raisins
¼ cup peanuts, dry-roasted
*   and powdered*
juice of 1 lime
handful of coriander leaves
salt to taste

Wash and dry eggplant. Cut halfway through. Mix all ingredients together and stuff into eggplants. In large skillet, heat ghee. Place spice sides of eggplants into ghee. Cover and cook on low flame till soft, turning occasionally. If burning occurs, add ½ cup water. Serves 8–10.

Eggplant Curry

10 Japanese eggplants,
cut 2–3 inches long
2 cups buttermilk
5 tablespoons ghee
1 teaspoon chickpea flour
2 green chilis, finely chopped
pinch of asafetida
½ teaspoon turmeric powder
1 teaspoon cumin powder
1 teaspoon coriander powder
1 teaspoon garam masala
1 teaspoon cumin seeds
handful of coriander leaves
salt to taste

Mix chickpea flour with buttermilk. Beat well. Cut eggplants into quarters, halfway through. Mix all powdered spices and stuff into each eggplant. In large skillet, heat ghee. Add cumin seeds, asafetida, and chilis. When brown, put in eggplants. Fry 5 minutes. Pour in buttermilk and remaining ingredients. Cover and cook on low flame till soft. Garnish with coriander leaves. Serves 8–10.

Eggplant & Potatoes

2 medium eggplants, cubed
2 medium potatoes, peeled and diced
2 large tomatoes, blanched and sliced

2 green chilis, finely sliced
1-inch piece ginger root, grated
¼ cup grated coconut
handful coriander leaves
1-inch piece of cinnamon stick
a few peppercorns
3 tablespoons ghee
1 teaspoon mustard seeds
½ teaspoon turmeric powder
⅛ teaspoon asafetida
salt to taste

Grind ginger, chilis, coconut, cinnamon, and peppercorns into paste with a little water; set aside. In medium saucepan, heat ghee. Add mustard seeds and asafetida. When popping stops, add paste and mix well. Fry briefly. Mix in turmeric, salt, potatoes, and eggplant. Fry 5 minutes. Add tomato and 1 cup water and mix well. Cover and cook on low flame, stirring occasionally, till potatoes are soft. If mixture becomes too dry and starts to stick to pan, add 1 cup water or buttermilk. Mix well. Cover and cook till gravy is thick. Garnish with coriander leaves. Serves 8–10.

Beans & Coconut

2 cups chopped green beans (any type)
½ cup grated coconut
3 tablespoons ghee
1 green chili, finely chopped
½ teaspoon cumin powder
1 teaspoon coriander powder
pinch of asafetida
1 teaspoon turbinado sugar
½ teaspoon mustard seeds

a few curry leaves
handful of coriander leaves
salt to taste

In saucepan, heat ghee. Add mustard seeds and asafetida. When popping stops, add chili and beans. Mix and cover. Cook without water on low flame till soft. Mix in remaining ingredients with 1 cup water. Cook till dry. Garnish with coriander leaves. Serves 3–4.

Beans & Potatoes

2 cups chopped beans (any type)
2 cups potatoes, diced
2 medium tomatoes, blanched and sliced
4 tablespoons ghee
1 green chili, finely chopped
1-inch piece ginger root, grated
1 teaspoon turmeric powder
1 teaspoon cumin seeds
½ teaspoon mustard seeds
pinch of asafetida
1 teaspoon coriander powder
handful of coriander leaves
salt to taste

In large skillet, heat ghee. Add cumin seeds, mustard seeds, and asafetida. When popping stops, add chili and ginger and fry briefly. Add potatoes and turmeric and mix well. Fry for 3–5 minutes. Add beans and 1 cup water. Cover and cook on low flame till soft. Add remaining ingredients. Cook till dry. Garnish with coriander leaves. Serves 5–6.

Beans & Buttermilk

2 cups chopped beans (any type)
2 cups buttermilk
1 tablespoon grated coconut
1 green chili, finely chopped
½-inch piece ginger root, grated
3 tablespoons ghee
1 teaspoon cumin seeds
½ teaspoon mustard seeds
pinch of asafetida
½ teaspoon turmeric powder
1 teaspoon garam masala
handful of coriander leaves
salt to taste

In saucepan, heat ghee. Add cumin seeds, mustard seeds, and asafetida. When popping stops, add chili and ginger and fry briefly. Add beans and turmeric. Cover and cook without water on low flame till soft. Add remaining ingredients. Cook till gravy is thick. Garnish with coriander leaves. Serves 3–4.

Beans & Curd

2 cups chopped beans (any type)
4 cups milk
3 tablespoons ghee
1 green chili, finely chopped
½ teaspoon fenugreek seeds
½ teaspoon cumin seeds
½ teaspoon mustard seeds
½ teaspoon turmeric powder
½ teaspoon garam masala

pinch of asafetida
handful of coriander leaves
salt to taste

Make milk into curd. Press for 20 minutes, then cut into 1-inch cubes. Set aside. In saucepan, heat ghee. Add cumin seeds, mustard seeds, and fenugreek seeds. When popping stops, add asafetida and chili and fry briefly. Add beans and turmeric powder. Mix well. Cover and cook on low flame till beans are soft. Add remaining ingredients with ½ cup water and mix well. Cook 3–5 minutes. Garnish with coriander leaves. Serves 4–5.

Green Papaya & Coconut

1 medium green papaya
1 teaspoon urad dal
½ cup grated coconut
2 tablespoons ghee
1 green chili, finely chopped
handful coriander leaves
1 teaspoon mustard seeds
½ teaspoon turmeric powder
salt to taste

Peel papaya and cut into small pieces. In skillet, heat ghee. Add chilis, mustard seeds, and *dal.* Cook till *dal* turns red. Add coconut, turmeric, papaya, and salt. Cover tightly and cook without water on low flame, stirring occasionally, till soft. Garnish with coriander leaves. Serves 3–4.

Papaya Curry

1 medium green papaya, peeled and diced

1 large tomato, blanched and sliced
½ cup garbanzo beans
1 cup yogurt, beaten with 1 cup water
1 green chili, finely chopped
½-inch piece ginger root, grated
3 tablespoons ghee
1 teaspoon cumin seeds, dry-roasted
    and powdered
2 bay leaves
½ teaspoon turmeric powder
1 teaspoon garam masala
salt to taste

Soak garbanzo beans overnight in 4 cups water. In morning, boil in same water till soft. Drain and set aside. In saucepan, heat ghee. Add chilis, ginger, and bay leaves and fry briefly. Add papaya. Mix well. Cover and cook on low flame for 5–10 minutes. Add rest of ingredients except *garam masala*. With a cup of water, cook down till gravy is thick. Mix in *garam masala*. Serves 4–5.

Green Papaya & Tomatoes

1 large green papaya, peeled and
    cut into small pieces
2 large tomatoes, blanched and peeled
1 cup grated coconut
1 green chili
1-inch piece ginger root
3 tablespoons ghee
1 teaspoon cumin seeds
5 peppercorns
½ teaspoon turmeric powder
2 pinches asafetida
salt to taste

Grind coconut, peppercorns, chili, cumin seeds, and ginger into paste with a little water. In saucepan, heat ghee. Add paste, asafetida, and turmeric and mix well. Cook till light brown. Add salt and papaya. Mix well. Fry for 3–5 minutes. Add tomatoes and 2 cups water. Cover and cook on low flame till papaya is quite soft. This preparation should be a bit liquidy. Serves 5–6.

Papaya in Yogurt Gravy

> 1 medium green papaya,
>   peeled and diced
> 2 large tomatoes, blanched and sliced
> 1 cup yogurt, beaten with 1 cup water
> 1 green chili
> 2 tablespoons ghee
> 1 teaspoon cumin seeds
> 3 bay leaves
> ½ teaspoon turmeric powder
> ½ teaspoon turbinado sugar
> 1 teaspoon garam masala
> 1-inch piece ginger root
> salt to taste

Grind ginger, chili, and cumin seeds into paste. In large skillet, heat ghee. Add bay leaves, ginger paste, and diced papaya and mix well. Fry for 5–7 minutes. Add tomatoes, salt, sugar, and all spices except *garam masala*. Cook till dry. Add beaten yogurt and cook on low flame till thick. Mix in *garam masala*. Serves 4–5.

Green Peas & Yogurt

> 3 cups green peas (shelled)
> 1 cup yogurt, well beaten

1 green chili, finely chopped
1-inch piece ginger root, grated
3 tablespoons ghee
1 teaspoon coriander powder
½ teaspoon turmeric powder
pinch of asafetida
handful of coriander leaves
salt to taste

Grind ginger, chili, coriander, and turmeric into paste. In saucepan, boil peas in water till soft; drain and set aside. In skillet, heat ghee. Add asafetida and fry briefly. Add paste and fry 1–2 minutes. Add peas, mix well, and cook 5–10 minutes on low flame. Mix in beaten yogurt. Cook a few minutes. Garnish with coriander leaves. Serves 4–5.

Green Peas & Curd

4 cups green peas (shelled)
4 cups milk
2 green chilis, finely chopped
½-inch piece ginger root, grated
2 tablespoons ghee
½ teaspoon cumin seeds
6 peppercorns
⅛ teaspoon asafetida
1 teaspoon coriander powder
½ teaspoon turmeric powder
juice of 1 lime
handful of coriander leaves
salt to taste

In saucepan, heat milk till boiling. Add citric acid or lemon juice to make curd. Strain curd in cheesecloth or muslin cloth. Tie and put under a heavy weight for 20–30 minutes to press out liquid. Slice into 1-inch cubes. Deep-fry in hot ghee till lightly browned; drain and set aside. Grind into paste coriander leaves, cumin seeds, peppercorns, chilis, and ginger; set aside. In saucepan, boil peas in 3 cups water till soft; drain and set aside. In skillet, heat ghee. Add asafetida and paste and mix well. Fry briefly. Add turmeric, salt, lime juice, and peas with 1 cup water. Cook till gravy forms. Add fried curd. Cook 2–3 minutes. Garnish with coriander leaves. Serves 6–7.

Green Peas & Tomatoes

3 cups green peas, shelled
5 large tomatoes, blanched and peeled
2 tablespoons ghee
1 green chili, finely chopped
½-inch piece ginger root, grated
1 teaspoon black pepper powder
salt to taste

Grind into paste ginger and chilis. In frying pan, heat ghee. Add paste and fry briefly. Add peas and salt with 1 cup water. Cover and cook on low flame till soft. Add tomatoes and black pepper. Cook 5–10 minutes. Serves 4–5.

Green Peas & Bell Peppers

3 cups green peas (shelled or frozen)
2 large bell peppers, finely chopped
¼ cup grated coconut
3 tablespoons ghee
1 green chili
½-inch piece ginger root

⅛ teaspoon asafetida
½ teaspoon cinnamon powder
salt to taste

Grind into paste chili, ginger, and coconut. In skillet, heat ghee. Add asafetida and paste and mix well. Fry briefly. Add peppers and salt. Fry till peppers change color. Add peas and 1 cup water and mix well. Cover and cook on low flame till soft (add more water if necessary.) When water is evaporated, remove from heat. Garnish with cinnamon powder. Serves 4–5.

Green Peas & Curd

4 cups green peas, shelled
4 cups milk
1 green chili, finely chopped
2 tablespoons ghee
1 teaspoon cumin seeds
½ teaspoon garam masala
½ teaspoon turmeric powder
pinch of asafetida
salt to taste

In saucepan, bring milk to boil. Curdle with lemon juice or citric acid. Wash cheese through muslin cloth, hang for 20 minutes, then crumble. Set aside. In skillet, heat ghee. Add cumin seeds. When brown, add asafetida and chili and fry briefly. Add peas, turmeric, salt, and 2 cups water and mix well. Cook till soft. Mix in rest of ingredients. Cook till dry. Serves 5–6.

Green Peppers & Green Mango

6 large peppers

2 medium green mangoes
1 cup grated coconut
4 tablespoons ghee
1 green chili, finely chopped
1 teaspoon turbinado sugar
1-inch piece of ginger root, grated
⅛ teaspoon asafetida
salt to taste

Wash peppers and slit them down the side without splitting. Remove seeds. Peel and slice mangoes, removing pits. Make into paste mango, chili, ginger, coconut, salt, and sugar. Stuff paste equally into peppers. In skillet, heat ghee. Add peppers, cover, and cook on low flame. After 5 minutes, turn over. Cook till all skin on peppers has changed color. Serves 6.

Stuffed Peppers

6 medium green peppers
1 cup chickpea flour
3 cups coconut milk or water
8 tablespoons ghee
1 cup grated coconut
2 chilis, finely chopped
1-inch piece ginger root, grated
1 teaspoon garam masala
1 teaspoon cumin seeds
1 tablespoon coriander powder
⅛ teaspoon asafetida
salt to taste

Slit peppers halfway through on one side and remove seeds without breaking pepper. Set aside. In frying pan, heat 2 tablespoons ghee. Add chickpea flour, mix well, and fry on medium flame till red in color; set aside. In frying pan, heat 4 tablespoons ghee. Add chilis and ginger and cook till light brown. Add all spices and chick-pea flour and mix well. Cook briefly. Remove from flame, then stuff into peppers equally. In skillet, heat 4 tablespoons ghee and fry stuffed peppers on low flame, turning gently till color changes. Add coconut milk. Cover and cook till peppers are tender and there is a thick gravy. Garnish with grated coconut. Serves 6.

Green Peppers & Yogurt

4 large green peppers, diced
¼ cup grated coconut
1 cup yogurt, beaten
   with 1 cup water
1 green chili, finely chopped
1-inch piece ginger root, grated
2 tablespoons ghee
1 teaspoon cumin seeds
½ teaspoon garam masala
½ teaspoon turmeric powder
⅛ teaspoon asafetida
handful of coriander leaves
salt to taste

Make into paste ginger, chili, and coconut. In skillet, heat ghee. Add cumin seeds and asafetida and mix well. When light brown, add paste and fry briefly. Stir in peppers, and fry till light red in color. Mix in yogurt, spices, and salt. Cook till peppers are quite tender and gravy is thick. Garnish with coriander leaves. Serves 4–5.

Green Peppers (Fancy Style)

4 large green peppers, finely chopped

¼ peanuts, dry-roasted and pounded
¼ cup raisins
¼ cup grated coconut
½ teaspoon mustard seeds
3 tablespoons ghee
1 teaspoon garam masala
¼ teaspoon red chili powder
½ teaspoon turmeric powder
handful of coriander leaves
salt to taste

In saucepan, heat ghee. Add mustard seeds and asafetida. When popping stops, add peppers and mix well. Fry till color changes. Add turmeric and 1 cup water. Cover and cook till quite soft. Mix in all other ingredients except coriander leaves. Fry briefly. Garnish with coriander leaves. Serves 4–5.

Peppers Stuffed with Potatoes

8 medium green peppers
2 large potatoes, boiled,
 peeled, and mashed
2 green chilis, finely chopped
½-inch piece ginger root, grated
5 tablespoons ghee
1 teaspoon cumin powder
1 teaspoon coriander powder
½ teaspoon turmeric powder
½ teaspoon garam masala
juice of 1 lime
handful of coriander leaves
salt to taste

Wash and dry peppers. Slice halfway through, carefully removing seeds. Mix all ingredients together and stuff into peppers. In skillet, heat ghee. Add peppers. Fry on medium flame for 5 minutes. Cover and cook on low flame, turning occasionally, till soft. Two cups of crumbled curd may be used instead of potatoes. Serves 8.

Spiced Peppers

2½ cups green peppers, diced
1 tablespoon grated coconut
3 tablespoons ghee
½ teaspoon mustard seeds
½ teaspoon turmeric powder
½ teaspoon garam masala
⅛ teaspoon asafetida
salt to taste

In skillet, heat ghee. Add mustard seeds and asafetida. When popping stops, add peppers and mix well. Fry till color changes. Add all spices. Mix well, cover, and cook on low flame till soft. Serves 4–6.

Fried Peppers & Potatoes

3 cups peppers, sliced
2 medium potatoes, diced
1 cup buttermilk
1 green chili, finely chopped
2 tablespoons ghee
1 teaspoon cumin seeds
½ teaspoon mustard seeds
½ teaspoon turmeric powder
½ teaspoon coriander powder

½ teaspoon garam masala
½ teaspoon black peppers
salt to taste

Deep-fry peppers till brown; drain. Deep-fry potatoes till brown; drain. In skillet, heat ghee. Add cumin seeds, mustard seeds, and chili and mix well. When popping stops, add buttermilk and all spices. Mix well. Cook 1–3 minutes. Add peppers and potatoes. Cook on low flame till gravy is thick. Serves 6–8.

Toora Dal Kofta

1 cup toora dal
1 green chili
pinch of asafetida
salt to taste
ghee for deep frying

SAUCE:
2 cups yogurt, beaten
    with 2 cups water
1 green chili
3 tablespoons ghee
½ cup grated coconut
1-inch piece ginger root, grated
1 teaspoon cumin seeds
1 teaspoon coriander seeds
¼ teaspoon fenugreek seeds
½ teaspoon mustard seeds
handful of coriander leaves
salt to taste

Soak *dal* for 1–3 hours. Drain and grind into paste with chili, asafetida, and salt. Roll into 1-inch balls and deep-fry in ghee till brown;

drain. (NOTE: Fry 1 ball first; if it breaks apart, add ½ cup chick-pea flour.) For sauce: in frying pan, dry-roast all spices except mustard and grind into paste with coconut, ginger, chili, and salt. A little water may be added. Set aside. In saucepan, heat ghee. Add mustard seeds. When popping stops, add paste and fry briefly. Add yogurt to sauce, mixing well. Bring to full boil. Remove from heat and add *kofta* balls. Garnish with coriander leaves. Serves 4–6.

Channa Dal Kofta

1 cup channa dal
1-inch piece ginger root, grated
1 tablespoon grated coconut
pinch of asafetida
a few raisins
handful of coriander leaves, minced
salt to taste
ghee for deep frying

SAUCE:
2 cups baby potatoes, boiled and peeled
4 cups coconut milk or buttermilk
2 tablespoons ghee
2 green chilis, sliced
1-inch piece ginger root, grated
1 cup tomato, blanched and sliced
½ teaspoon turmeric powder
1 teaspoon garam masala
⅛ teaspoon asafetida
a few coriander leaves
salt to taste

Soak *dal* in water overnight. Drain and grind into paste with all *kofta* ingredients except raisins. Roll into 1-inch balls and put a raisin in the center of each. Deep-fry in ghee till brown. Drain and set aside. (NOTE: Fry one ball first; if it breaks apart, add ½ cup chickpea flour.) In saucepan, heat ghee. Add chilis, ginger, and asafetida and fry briefly. Add tomato and turmeric. When liquidy, add all other ingredients, mix well, and bring to boil. Add *kofta*. Cook 1 minute, then remove from flame. Garnish with coriander leaves. Serves 4–5.

Zucchini Kofta

4 cups zucchini, grated
¼ cup chickpea flour
½ teaspoon cayenne pepper
½-inch piece ginger root, grated
1 teaspoon cumin powder
⅛ teaspoon asafetida
handful of coriander leaves, minced
salt to taste
ghee for deep frying

SAUCE:
3 cups tomato, blanched
¼ cup grated coconut
¼ cup yogurt, beaten
3 tablespoons ghee
1 green chili
1-inch piece ginger root
1 tablespoon poppy seeds
pinch of asafetida
½ teaspoon turmeric powder
½ teaspoon coriander powder
½ teaspoon cumin powder
½ teaspoon garam masala

handful coriander leaves
salt to taste

Mix all *kofta* ingredients together. Roll into 1-inch balls and deep-fry in ghee till brown; drain. Set aside. Grind into paste poppy seeds, ginger, chili, coconut, and asafetida. In saucepan, heat ghee. Add paste. Cook till brown. Add all other ingredients and mix well. Cook till dry. Add *kofta*. Cover with 4 cups water and mix carefully. Cook on low flame for 5 minutes. Garnish with coriander leaves. Serves 6–7.

Potato Kofta

2 cups potatoes, boiled,
  peeled, and sliced
½ cup chickpea flour
2 green chilis, finely chopped
1 teaspoon cumin powder
pinch of baking powder
½ teaspoon turmeric powder
pinch of asafetida
1 teaspoon crushed pomegranate
  seeds (optional)
handful of coriander leaves
salt to taste
ghee for deep frying

SAUCE:
2 cups tomato, blanched
  and sliced
2 cups yogurt, beaten with 2 cups water
1 cup coconut milk or water
3 tablespoons ghee
1 green chili, finely chopped

½-inch piece ginger root, grated
½ teaspoon turmeric powder
⅛ teaspoon asafetida
1 teaspoon coriander powder
1 teaspoon cumin powder
1 teaspoon garam masala
handful of coriander leaves
salt to taste

Mix cumin powder, turmeric, baking powder, salt, and chickpea flour. Add enough buttermilk to form a thick batter. Mash potatoes with remaining *kofta* ingredients till smooth. Roll into 1-inch balls. Dip in chickpea flour. Deep-fry in ghee till brown. Drain and set aside. In saucepan, heat ghee. Add chilis, ginger, and asafetida. Fry till color changes. Add all spices. Mix well and add tomato. Cook till dry. Add *kofta* and yogurt and mix carefully. Bring to boil. Remove from heat. Garnish with coriander leaves. Serves 5–7.

Curd Kofta

2 cups 1-inch curd cubes
1 cup chickpea flour
½ teaspoon turmeric powder
pinch of asafetida
½ teaspoon chili powder
salt to taste
ghee for deep frying

SAUCE:
½ cup grated coconut
2 teaspoons poppy seeds
2 tablespoons ghee
1 green chili, finely chopped
1-inch piece ginger root, grated

2 cups yogurt, beaten
2 teaspoons coriander seeds
8 almonds, chopped
4 cloves
¼ teaspoon cardamon powder
handful of coriander leaves
salt to taste

Mix chickpea flour and spices, adding enough buttermilk to form a thick batter. Cover each curd cube with batter and deep-fry in ghee till brown. Drain and set aside. In frying pan, dry-roast all spices and grind into paste with coconut, ginger, and chilis. A little water may be added. In saucepan, heat ghee. Add paste and fry till brown, then add yogurt and salt and bring to boil. Add curd and mix carefully. Remove from flame and garnish with coriander leaves. (Instead of yogurt, 3 cups blended tomato may be used, but you must cook tomato 5 minutes before adding curd.) Serves 4–5.

Banana Kofta

4 large green bananas,
*   peeled and boiled*
4 tablespoons chickpea flour
2 green chilis, finely chopped
1 teaspoon cumin seeds, dry-roasted
*   and powdered*
1 teaspoon sugar
½-inch piece ginger root, grated
2 pinches asafetida
juice of 1 lime
handful of coriander leaves
salt to taste
ghee for deep frying

SAUCE:

3 cups yogurt, beaten with
   3 cups water
3 tablespoons ghee
1 green chili, finely chopped
½-inch piece ginger root, grated
⅛ teaspoon asafetida
2 bay leaves
½ teaspoon cumin seeds
1 teaspoon cumin seeds,
   dry-roasted and powdered
1 teaspoon garam masala
1 teaspoon turmeric powder
handful of coriander leaves
salt to taste

Mix together all *kofta* ingredients, kneading till nicely mixed. Take small amounts and press lightly in hand to make 2-inch rounds, placing on greased pan till all mixture is rolled out. Deep-fry in ghee till *koftas* are floating on top of ghee and golden brown. Drain and put in baking pan. In saucepan, heat ghee. Add cumin seeds, bay leaves, and asafetida, and fry till golden brown. Add chilis and ginger, and fry briefly. Add all other spices. Add yogurt. Cook 3–5 minutes on low flame. Pour over *kofta*. Garnish with coriander leaves. Serves 4–6.

Fried Okra

3 cups okra, cut into small pieces
2 green chilis, finely chopped
3 tablespoons ghee
½ teaspoon mustard seeds
¼ teaspoon turmeric powder
⅛ teaspoon asafetida

a few curry leaves
salt to taste

In skillet, heat ghee. Add mustard seeds, chilis, and asafetida. When popping stops, add okra and curry leaves. When color changes, add all other ingredients and mix well. Cook over slow flame for 5 minutes, stirring occasionally to avoid sticking. Serves 4–6.

Stuffed Okra

15–20 large okra
4 tablespoons chickpea flour
¼ cup grated coconut
6 tablespoons ghee
1 green chili, finely chopped
1-inch piece ginger root, grated
1 tablespoon coriander powder
1 teaspoon cumin powder
½ teaspoon turmeric powder
pinch of asafetida
salt to taste

Slice okra halfway through. Set aside. In frying pan, heat 2 tablespoons ghee. Remove from flame. Add all ingredients. Mix well for a few minutes. Stuff this mixture into okra. In frying pan, heat 4 tablespoons ghee. Add stuffed okra and fry till red and crisp. Drain. Serves 6–7.

Okra & Dal

1½ cups sliced okra
1 cup channa dal
4 tablespoons ghee

1 green chili, finely chopped
1-inch piece ginger root, grated
½ teaspoon turmeric powder
1 teaspoon cumin seeds
1 teaspoon coriander seeds
¼ cup grated coconut
handful of coriander leaves
salt to taste

Soak *dal* overnight in 4 cups water. In saucepan, boil in soaking water till soft; set aside. In skillet, heat 2 tablespoons ghee. Add ginger, cumin seeds, coriander seeds, chili, and coconut. When color changes, remove from heat. Grind all spices into a paste. Heat 2 tablespoons ghee. Add paste, *dal,* and okra and mix well. Cook till gravy turns thick. Serves 4–5.

Okra & Tomatoes

20 medium okra
3 large tomatoes, blanched and sliced
5 tablespoons ghee
1-inch piece ginger root, grated
1 green chili, finely chopped
½ teaspoon turmeric powder
1 teaspoon cumin seeds
¼ teaspoon asafetida
handful of coriander leaves
salt to taste

Wash and cut off both ends of okra. Then slice in half lengthwise. In skillet, heat 3 tablespoons ghee. Add okra. Cook till brown. Remove and heat 2 tablespoons ghee. Add cumin seeds and asafetida. When brown, add ginger and chili, then mix well. Fry briefly.

Add tomato, salt, and turmeric with 1 cup of water. When thick add okra. Cook a few minutes. Garnish with coriander leaves. Serves 6–8.

Okra & Yogurt

15–20 medium okra
1 cup yogurt
3 tablespoons ghee
1 green chili, finely chopped
1-inch piece ginger root, grated
1 teaspoon cumin seeds
⅛ teaspoon asafetida
handful of coriander leaves
1 teaspoon salt

Grind into paste ginger, chilis, asafetida, and coriander. Cut both ends off okra. Slice down middle halfway through. Stuff paste into the okra. In large frying pan, heat ghee. Add okra and fry briefly. Add turmeric and salt. Cover and cook on low flame till soft, stirring occasionally, then add yogurt. Cook a few minutes. Garnish with coriander leaves. Serves 6–8.

Okra Curry

15–20 slitted okra (remove insides)
1 cup buttermilk
3 tablespoons ghee
1 teaspoon chickpea flour
2 green chilis
1-inch piece ginger root
pinch of asafetida
1 teaspoon cumin powder

1 teaspoon coriander powder
1 teaspoon turmeric powder
handful of coriander leaves
salt to taste

Grind ginger and chilis into paste. Mix in all spices and equally stuff each okra. Beat chickpea flour into buttermilk till smooth. In frying pan, heat ghee. Add okra and fry till light brown. Add buttermilk and cook till thick. Garnish with coriander leaves. Serves 6–8.

Okra & Potatoes

20–25 large okra
2 medium potatoes, diced
1 large tomato, blanched and sliced
3 tablespoons ghee
1 green chili, finely chopped
½-inch piece ginger root, grated
½ teaspoon panchphoron
½ teaspoon turmeric powder
pinch of asafetida
1 teaspoon cumin seeds,
    dry-roasted and powdered
handful of coriander leaves
salt to taste

In skillet, heat ghee. Add *panchphoron* and asafetida. When popping stops, add chili and ginger and mix well. Fry briefly. Add potatoes and okra and fry, stirring occasionally, till color changes. Add remaining ingredients with ½ cup water. Mix well. Cover and cook on low flame till soft. Garnish with coriander leaves. Serves 8–10.

Okra with Mustard

25–30 medium okra, sliced halfway through
2 medium tomatoes, blanched and sliced
3 tablespoons ghee
1 green chili, finely chopped
½ teaspoon cumin seeds
¼ teaspoon fenugreek seeds
½ teaspoon turmeric powder
2 tablespoons mustard powder
salt to taste

In saucepan, heat ghee. Add cumin seeds, fenugreek seeds, and chili. When slightly brown, add mustard powder and fry briefly. Add okra, mixing well. When color changes, add tomato, turmeric, and salt. Mix well. Add 1 cup water. Cover and cook on low flame for 3–5 minutes. Serves 8–10.

Pineapple in Buttermilk Sauce

1 medium pineapple, peeled and diced
1 cup buttermilk
½ cup grated coconut
2 green chilis, finely chopped
2 tablespoons ghee
1 teaspoon cumin seeds
½ teaspoon mustard seeds
½ teaspoon turmeric powder
½ teaspoon fenugreek seeds, crushed
salt to taste

Grind into paste chilis, coconut, and cumin seeds with a little water. In saucepan, put pineapple, turmeric, and salt with 2 cups water.

Cover and cook on low flame till pineapple is soft. In skillet, heat ghee. Add mustard seeds and fenugreek seeds. When popping stops, add paste and mix well. Cook and stir for a few minutes. Add pine-apple and cook till dry, then add buttermilk. Cook 3–5 minutes on low flame. Serves 6–8.

Fried Pineapple

1 large pineapple, peeled and diced
¼ cup grated coconut
1 green chili, finely chopped
½-inch piece ginger root, grated
3 tablespoons ghee
1 teaspoon mustard seeds
1 teaspoon turbinado sugar
handful of coriander leaves
salt to taste

In saucepan, heat ghee. Add mustard seeds. When popping stops, add ginger and chili and fry briefly. Add pineapple and salt. Cover and cook on low flame till soft (1 cup water may be added.) Add sugar and coconut and mix well. Garnish with coriander leaves. Serves 6–8.

Spiced Pineapple

1 medium pineapple, peeled and diced
½ cup grated coconut
2 green chilis, finely chopped
1-inch piece ginger root, grated
1 teaspoon poppy seeds
4 tablespoons ghee
½ teaspoon turmeric powder

1 teaspoon coriander powder
1 teaspoon cinnamon powder
¼ teaspoon cardamon powder
salt to taste

Grind all ingredients except pineapple into paste with a little water. In skillet, heat ghee. Add paste. Fry with ½ cup water till spices are smelling nice. Add pineapple and 1 cup water. Cover and cook on low flame till soft. Serves 5–7.

Fried Potatoes #1

2 large potatoes
¼ cup dry-roasted peanuts, pounded
1 tablespoon sesame seeds,
    dry-roasted and pounded
1 tablespoon mango powder (optional)
4 tablespoons ghee
1 teaspoon cumin powder
1 teaspoon coriander powder
¼ teaspoon chili powder
½ teaspoon garam masala
handful of coriander leaves
salt to taste

Peel potatoes and slice into fingers. Soak in water. Mix all powdered spices together. Roll each potato finger in spices till completely covered. In frying pan, heat ghee. Add potatoes and fry 3–5 minutes. Stir in 1 cup water. Mix well, cover, and cook on low flame, stirring occasionally, till soft. Mix in peanuts and sesame seed powder. Garnish with coriander leaves. Serves 4–5.

Fried Potatoes #2

*3 medium potatoes, peeled
    and cut into fingers
ghee for deep frying
1 teaspoon mango powder (optional)
1 teaspoon cumin powder
1 teaspoon coriander powder
½ teaspoon garam masala
pinch of asafetida
handful of coriander leaves
salt to taste*

Deep-fry potatoes till brown. Drain and mash. Mix in all ingredients with potatoes. Serves 3–4.

Potato & Eggplant Shak

*2½ cups potatoes, peeled and diced
1 large eggplant, thinly sliced
2 large tomatoes, blanched,
    peeled and sliced
4 tablespoons ghee
1 teaspoon coriander powder
1 teaspoon cumin powder
½ teaspoon turmeric powder
½ teaspoon garam masala
¼ teaspoon chili powder
salt to taste*

In skillet, heat ghee. Add tomatoes and all spices. When dry, add potatoes and eggplant and mix well. Fry for 3–5 minutes. Add 1½ cups water. Cover and cook on low flame till potatoes are soft. Serves 4–5.

Baby Potatoes & Tomatoes

3 cups potatoes, peeled and sliced
1 cup tomatoes, blanched and sliced
2 green chilis, finely chopped
1-inch piece ginger root, grated
3 tablespoons ghee
½ teaspoon mustard seeds
½ teaspoon turmeric powder
⅛ teaspoon asafetida
handful of coriander leaves
salt to taste

In skillet, heat ghee. Add mustard seeds and asafetida. When popping stops, add ginger and chilis, mix well, then fry briefly. Add turmeric, salt, and tomatoes and mix well. When dry, add potatoes. Fry 3–5 minutes, stirring constantly. Add 1½ cups water. Mix well, cover, and cook till potatoes are soft. Garnish with coriander leaves. Serves 4–5.

Sweet and Sour Potatoes

3 cups potatoes, peeled and cubed
2 green chilis, finely chopped
¼ cup honey
½ teaspoon mustard seeds
pinch of asafetida
4 tablespoons ghee
1 teaspoon cumin seeds
½ teaspoon turmeric powder

1 teaspoon cumin powder
1 teaspoon coriander powder
handful of coriander leaves
salt to taste

In skillet, heat ghee. Add cumin seeds, mustard seeds, and asafetida and mix well. When popping stops, add chilis and fry briefly. Add turmeric, salt, and potatoes, mix well, and fry for 3–5 minutes. Mix in all ingredients and fry again briefly. Add 1½ cups water. Cover and cook on low flame till potatoes are soft. Garnish with coriander leaves. Serves 4–5.

Fancy Potatoes

3 cups potatoes, peeled and cubed
¼ cup roasted peanuts, powdered
¼ cup powdered channa dal
1 cup sour yogurt, beaten with 1 cup water
2 green chilis, finely chopped
4 tablespoons ghee
1 tablespoon grated coconut
1-inch piece ginger root, grated
pinch of asafetida
1 teaspoon garam masala
1 teaspoon coriander powder
1 teaspoon cumin powder
handful of coriander leaves
salt to taste

In saucepan, heat ghee. Add asafetida, chili, and ginger and fry till brown. Add all spices and coconut, mix well, and fry briefly. Add potatoes, *dal,* and peanuts. Fry for 5–7 minutes. Add yogurt. Cover and cook on low flame till potatoes are soft. Garnish with coriander leaves. Serves 4–6.

Masala Potatoes

6 large potatoes, peeled and cubed
1 cup grated coconut
4 tablespoons ghee
2 green chilis, finely chopped
1 tablespoon cumin powder
1 tablespoon coriander powder
½ teaspoon turmeric powder
1 teaspoon mustard seeds
⅛ teaspoon asafetida
a few coriander leaves
salt to taste

In saucepan, heat ghee. Add mustard seeds and asafetida. When popping stops, add chilis, mix well, and fry briefly. Add turmeric, potatoes, and coconut, mix well, then fry for 5 minutes. Cover with water and mix in rest of ingredients. Cook till potatoes are soft. Add more water if too dry. Result should be thick and liquidy. Serves 6–7.

Potatoes & Peanuts

3 cup potatoes, diced
½ cup peanuts, ground
2 tablespoons grated coconut
1-inch piece ginger root, grated
3 tablespoons ghee
1 teaspoon cumin seeds
1 teaspoon cumin powder
1 tablespoon coriander powder
1 teaspoon garam masala
¼ teaspoon red chili powder
salt to taste

In skillet, heat ghee. Add cumin seeds and ginger. When brown, add potatoes, mix well, and fry on low flame till potatoes are soft. Add all other ingredients and fry 1 minute, stirring occasionally. (1½ cups water can be added if sticking.) Serves 5–6.

Potatoes & Yogurt

6 cups potatoes, boiled, peeled, and halved
2 cups yogurt, beaten with 2 cups water
2 dried red chilis, crushed
3 tablespoons ghee
1 teaspoon cumin seeds
1 teaspoon turmeric powder
1 teaspoon garam masala
1 teaspoon ginger powder
⅛ teaspoon asafetida
handful of coriander leaves
salt to taste

In saucepan, heat ghee. Add chilis, cumin, and asafetida and fry till brown. Add turmeric powder and potatoes and mix well. Fry 5 minutes. Add all spices and beaten yogurt. Mix well. Cover and cook on low flame till gravy is thick and potatoes are soft. Garnish with coriander leaves. Serves 7–9.

Potatoes & Peas

4 cups potatoes, diced
1 cup green peas, shelled or frozen
¼ cup grated coconut
¼ cup cashews
2 green chilis
1-inch piece ginger root

4 tablespoons ghee
1 teaspoon poppy seeds
⅛ teaspoon asafetida
1 teaspoon cumin powder
1 teaspoon coriander powder
½ teaspoon turmeric powder
handful of coriander leaves
salt to taste

Grind into paste cashews, poppy seeds, chilis, ginger, and coconut. In saucepan, heat ghee. Add paste and asafetida and mix well. When brown, add all spices, potatoes, and peas and fry briefly. Add 2 cups water and mix well. Cover and cook on low flame till potatoes are soft. Serves 6–8.

Potatoes & Curd

3 cups potatoes, grated
4 cups milk
¼ cup peanuts, ground
2 green chilis, finely chopped
3 tablespoons ghee
1 teaspoon cumin seeds
handful of coriander leaves
salt to taste

In saucepan, bring milk to boil. Curdle with 2–3 tablespoons lemon juice or ¼ teaspoon citric acid. Wash and let strain through muslin cloth for 10 minutes, then crumble. In medium frying pan, heat ghee. Add cumin seeds and chilis and fry briefly. Add potatoes and mix well. Cook for 3–5 minutes, stirring constantly. Add ½ cup water, curd, and peanuts. Cover and cook on low flame till potatoes are soft. Garnish with coriander leaves. Serves 5–6.

Pumpkin & Coconut

3 cups pumpkin, peeled and grated
½ cup grated coconut
3 tablespoons ghee
1 teaspoon mustard seeds
¼ teaspoon turmeric powder
½ teaspoon chili powder
handful of coriander leaves
salt to taste

In medium frying pan, heat ghee. Add mustard seeds. When popping stops, add all spices, mix well, and fry briefly. Mix in coconut and pumpkin. Cover and cook on low flame till pumpkin is soft. Garnish with coriander leaves. Serves 4–5.

Spiced Pumpkin

6 cups pumpkin, peeled and diced
¼ cup grated coconut
2 green chilis, finely chopped
½-inch piece ginger root, grated
5 tablespoons ghee
1 teaspoon sesame seeds
1 teaspoon poppy seeds
pinch of asafetida
1 teaspoon mustard seeds
½ teaspoon turmeric powder
1 tablespoon turbinado sugar
*   (optional)*
handful of coriander leaves
salt to taste

In frying pan, heat 2 tablespoons ghee. Add coconut, sesame seeds, and poppy seeds and mix well. Cook till reddish. Grind into paste with a little water. In skillet, heat 3 tablespoons ghee. Add mustard seeds and asafetida. When popping stops, add pumpkin, chilis, turmeric, 1 cup water, and salt. Mix well. Cover and cook on low flame till soft. Mix in remaining ingredients. Garnish with coriander leaves. Serves 6–8.

Creamy Pumpkin

2 cups pumpkin, sliced
1 cup cream
1 green chili, finely chopped
3 tablespoons ghee
½ teaspoon turmeric powder
1 teaspoon cumin seeds
2 bay leaves
½ teaspoon cinnamon powder
1 teaspoon turbinado sugar
    (optional)
handful of coriander leaves
salt to taste

In saucepan, heat ghee. Add cumin seeds and bay leaves. When light brown, add chili and pumpkin. Mix well. Add all ingredients except coriander leaves. Cover and cook on low flame till soft and gravy is creamy. Garnish with coriander leaves. Serves 4–5.

Heavenly Pumpkin

3 cups pumpkin, sliced
2 cups milk
¼ cup grated coconut

1 green chili, finely chopped
3 tablespoons ghee
½ teaspoon cumin seeds
2 bay leaves
½ teaspoon turmeric powder
¼ teaspoon cinnamon powder
¼ teaspoon nutmeg powder
1 teaspoon garam masala
salt to taste

In saucepan, heat ghee. Add cumin seeds and bay leaves. When brown, add coconut and chili, mix well, and fry briefly. Add pumpkin and all ingredients except *garam masala*. Add ½ cup water and mix well. Cover and cook on low flame till soft. Mash to a creamy consistency and garnish with *garam masala*. Serves 4–6.

Fried Spinach

4 cups spinach, finely chopped
1 green chili, finely chopped
2 tablespoons ghee
pinch of asafetida
pinch of soda
½ teaspoon turmeric powder
salt to taste

Wash spinach 3 or 4 times. Mix in soda and drain. In skillet, heat ghee. Add cumin seeds and asafetida. When brown, add chilis and fry briefly. Add spinach, turmeric, and salt and mix well. Cover and cook on low flame till spinach has wilted. Serves 3–4.

Spinach & Fried Curd

5 cups spinach, finely chopped

8 cups milk
ghee for deep frying
3 tablespoons ghee
1 green chili, finely chopped
1-inch piece ginger root, grated
½ teaspoon cumin seeds
6 peppercorns
pinch of asafetida
1 tablespoon poppy seeds
½ teaspoon turmeric powder
1 teaspoon mango powder
   (optional)
salt to taste

In saucepan, bring milk to boil. Curdle with lemon juice or citric acid. Wash and press with heavy weight in cheese cloth for 30 minutes. Cut into 1-inch cubes. Deep-fry cubes till brown; drain. Wash spinach 3 or 4 times. Grind into paste spinach and poppy seeds. Set aside. Grind into paste chilis, peppercorns, ginger, and cumin seeds. In large frying pan, heat ghee. Add asafetida and turmeric and fry briefly. Add spice paste and ½ cup water. Mix well and fry a few minutes. Mix in spinach paste and 1 cup water. Cook on medium heat till boiling. Add mango powder and curd. Mix and cook till thick. Serves 5–7.

Fried Sweet Potatoes

6 sweet potatoes, peeled and grated
ghee for deep frying
¼ cup grated coconut
1 green chili, finely chopped
½ teaspoon garam masala
pinch of asafetida

handful of coriander leaves
salt to taste

Deep-fry potatoes till brown and crisp; drain. Carefully combine and mix all ingredients in mixing bowl. Coconut powder may be sprinkled on top. Serves 5–6.

Sweet Potatoes & Peanuts

5 sweet potatoes
½ cup peanuts, dry-roasted
and pounded
1 tablespoon sesame seeds,
dry-roasted and pounded
2 green chilis, finely chopped
1-inch piece ginger root, grated
2 tablespoons ghee
1 teaspoon garam masala
juice of 1 lime
salt to taste

Peel potatoes and cut in cubes. Boil in water with lime juice till soft. Drain and mash. In frying pan, heat ghee. Add chilis and ginger. When brown, add potatoes and all ingredients and mix well. Cook 5 minutes, stirring constantly. Serves 5–6.

Hot Sweet Potatoes

5 sweet potatoes
¼ cup grated coconut
¼ cup yellow mung dal,
dry-roasted and pounded
2 green chilis

1-inch piece ginger root
pinch of asafetida
1 teaspoon turbinado sugar
juice of 1 lime
½ teaspoon turmeric powder
4 tablespoons ghee
salt to taste

Peel potatoes and cut into long slices. Grind all other ingredients into paste. Stuff paste between 2 slices of potato and tie with string. Heat ghee. Add slices, cover, and cook on low flame, turning occasionally till potatoes are brown on both sides.

ALTERNATIVE: bake at 350°F or 177°C for 15–20 minutes. Serves 5–6.

Sweet Potatoes (North Indian)

5 sweet potatoes, peeled and grated
¼ cup peanuts, pounded
2 green chilis, finely chopped
½-inch piece ginger root,
*   grated*
½ teaspoon turmeric powder
juice of 1 lime
3 tablespoons ghee
1 teaspoon cumin seeds
½ teaspoon mustard seeds
⅛ teaspoon asafetida
handful of coriander leaves
salt to taste

In saucepan, boil potatoes in 3 cups water with lime juice till soft; drain. In skillet, heat ghee. Add cumin seeds, mustard seeds, and asafetida. When popping stops, add chili and ginger, mix well, and fry briefly. Add all other ingredients (except coriander leaves) plus 1 cup water. Mix well. Cook on low flame till gravy is thick. Garnish with coriander leaves. Serves 5–6.

Sweet Potato Curry

5 sweet potatoes, peeled and diced
1 cup peas, shelled
1 cup buttermilk
½-inch piece ginger root, grated
juice of 1 lime
3 tablespoons ghee
⅛ teaspoon asafetida
1 tablespoon coriander powder
1 teaspoon cumin powder
1 teaspoon mustard seeds
½ teaspoon turmeric powder
handful of coriander leaves
salt to taste

In saucepan, boil potatoes in water with lime juice till soft; drain. In saucepan, heat ghee. Add mustard seeds. When popping stops, add ginger and asafetida and fry briefly. Add peas and all spices, mixing well. Add buttermilk. Cover and cook on low flame till peas are soft. Add potatoes and cook 3–5 minutes. Garnish with coriander leaves. Serves 6–7.

Tomato Shak

12 large tomatoes, blanched and sliced
1 green chili, finely chopped
1-inch piece ginger root, grated

4 tablespoons ghee
1 clove
1 bay leaf, crumpled
2 pinches cardamon powder
½ teaspoon turbinado sugar
¼ teaspoon turmeric powder
1 teaspoon cumin powder
1 teaspoon coriander powder
1 tablespoon poppy seeds
⅛ teaspoon asafetida
salt to taste

In saucepan, heat ghee. Add chili, ginger, poppy seeds, clove, bay leaf, and asafetida and mix well. Fry till light brown. Add rest of spices and fry briefly. Add tomato with ½ cup water. Cover and cook on low flame till tomato is soft and mushy. Serves 7–9.

Stuffed Tomatoes

10 medium tomatoes
2 tablespoons chickpea flour
1 tablespoon sesame seeds, roasted
¼ cup grated coconut
1 green chili
½-inch piece ginger root, grated
1 teaspoon cumin powder
1 teaspoon coriander powder
½ teaspoon garam masala
pinch of asafetida
salt to taste

Core tomatoes and carefully remove seeds and pulp, reserving pulp. Grind all other ingredients into paste. Mix in tomato pulp and stuff into each tomato equally. Put tomatoes in cupcake pan. Put cupcake pan in a baking pan, making sure cupcake pan fits comfortably. Put ½ inch of water in baking pan. Cover and put on stove or bake in oven till tomatoes are soft. Serves 10.

Spicy Tomatoes

10 medium tomatoes, quartered
1 tablespoon chickpea flour
1 green chili, finely chopped
½ teaspoon cumin seeds
3 tablespoons ghee
½ teaspoon mustard seeds
pinch of asafetida
¼ teaspoon fenugreek seeds,
    coarsely powdered
½ teaspoon turmeric powder
handful of coriander leaves
salt to taste

Blend chickpea flour with 1 cup water. In saucepan, heat ghee. Add mustard seeds, cumin seeds, fenugreek powder, and asafetida and mix well. When mixture turns red, add turmeric, salt, and tomatoes. Mix well. Add chickpea flour mixture. Cover and cook on low flame till thick. Serves 7–8.

Tomato Curry

10 medium tomatoes, blanched and sliced
2 cups yogurt, beaten with 2 cups water
1 green chili, finely chopped
½-inch piece ginger root, grated
2 tablespoons ghee

1 teaspoon mustard seeds
½ teaspoon turmeric powder
⅛ teaspoon asafetida
a few neem leaves
handful of coriander leaves
salt to taste

In saucepan, put tomato, yogurt, ginger, salt, turmeric powder and curry leaves and mix well. Cook on low flame till tomato becomes soft. Remove from heat. In frying pan, heat ghee. Add mustard seeds and asafetida. When popping stops, add tomato mix. Bring to boil, then lower heat. Cook 3–5 minutes. Serves 7–8.

Tomatoes & Peanuts

3 cups tomatoes, blanched and sliced
2 cups peanuts, dry-roasted
2 green chilis, finely chopped
2 tablespoons ghee
1 teaspoon cumin powder
1 teaspoon garam masala
handful of coriander leaves
salt to taste

Grind into paste peanuts and chilis. In saucepan, heat ghee. Add paste and fry briefly. Mix in all other ingredients except coriander leaves. Cover and cook on low flame till tomato is soft. Garnish with coriander leaves. Serves 5–7.

Tomato & Pea Curry

2 cups tomatoes, blanched and sliced
1 cup peas, shelled

2 tablespoons chickpea flour
2 cups sour buttermilk
1 green chili, finely chopped
½-inch piece ginger root, grated
2 tablespoons ghee
2 bay leaves
½ teaspoon turmeric powder
1 teaspoon coriander powder
½ teaspoon cumin powder
½ teaspoon garam masala
pinch of asafetida
handful of coriander leaves
salt to taste

Blend chickpea flour and buttermilk. In saucepan, heat ghee. Add chili, ginger, bay leaves, and asafetida and fry briefly. Add tomato, peas, turmeric powder, and salt and mix well. Fry till tomato is soft. Add buttermilk and all spices and cook till peas are soft. Garnish with coriander leaves. Serves 4–6.

Radish Rolls

4 cups white radish, finely grated
2 cups semolina flour or farina
1 cup garam flour
2 tablespoons yogurt
2 green chilis, finely chopped
1-inch piece ginger root, grated
½ teaspoon turmeric powder
⅛ teaspoon asafetida
3 tablespoons ghee
1 teaspoon mustard seeds
2 tablespoons grated coconut

handful of coriander leaves
salt to taste

Grind into paste ginger, chilis, and coriander leaves. Mix into a dough with all ingredients except mustard seeds and asafetida. Roll dough into long thin rolls. Cut to 8-inch length. Steam for 25–30 minutes. Cool and slice ¼ inch thick. In frying pan, heat ghee. Add mustard seeds and asafetida. When popping stops, add slices. Fry on both sides till brown. Serves 6–8.

White Radish & Potatoes

3 cups radish, sliced thin
3 medium potatoes, peeled and sliced thin
1 green chili, finely chopped
½-inch piece ginger root, grated
4 tablespoons ghee
½ teaspoon cumin seeds
½ teaspoon mustard seeds
⅛ teaspoon asafetida
1 teaspoon coriander powder
1 teaspoon garam masala
salt to taste

In skillet, heat ghee. Add cumin seeds, mustard seeds, and asafetida. When popping stops, add chili and ginger and mix well. Fry briefly. Add radish and potatoes. Mix well. Cover and cook on low flame 5 minutes. Add 2 cups water. Cook till soft. Add remaining ingredients. Cook 1–3 minutes. Serves 6–8.

Zucchini & Tomatoes

10 small zucchini, sliced

4 medium tomatoes,
blanched and sliced
1 green chili, finely chopped
4 tablespoons ghee
1 teaspoon cumin seeds
½ teaspoon turmeric powder
1 teaspoon coriander powder
½ teaspoon garam masala
⅛ teaspoon asafetida
handful of coriander leaves
salt to taste

In skillet, heat ghee. Add cumin seeds and asafetida. When brown, add chilis, turmeric powder, and zucchini and mix well. Cover and cook on low flame till almost done. Add tomato, coriander powder, *garam masala* and salt. Mix well and cook till zucchini is soft. Garnish with coriander leaves. Serves 6–8.

Zucchini & Bell Peppers

10 small zucchini, sliced
2 cups diced green peppers
2 medium tomatoes, blanched and sliced
1 green chili, finely chopped
½-inch piece ginger root, grated
3 tablespoons ghee
1 teaspoon cumin seeds
1 teaspoon ajwan seeds
½ teaspoon mustard seeds
a few fenugreek seeds
½ teaspoon black pepper
½ teaspoon turmeric powder
1 teaspoon garam masala

handful of coriander leaves
salt to taste

Heat ghee. Add cumin seeds, fenugreek seeds, ajwan seeds, and mustard seeds. When popping stops, add ginger, chilis, and green peppers and mix well. Fry till peppers have changed color. Add zucchini, turmeric powder, and salt. Mix well and cook covered on low flame till zucchini is done. Add remaining ingredients except coriander leaves. Mix well. Cook 2–3 minutes. Garnish with coriander leaves. Serves 6–8.

Zucchini & Potatoes

3 cups zucchini, peeled and cubed
3 medium potatoes, peeled and cubed
1 green chili, finely chopped
3 tablespoons ghee
1 cup poppy seeds
½ teaspoon black cumin
½ teaspoon turmeric powder
¼ teaspoon ginger powder
salt to taste

Grind poppy seeds into paste with a little water. This can be done in a blender or spice grinder. Heat ghee. Add black cumin, potatoes, and turmeric powder. Fry 2–3 minutes. Add zucchini, 1 cup water, and all other ingredients except poppy seed paste. Mix well. Cover and cook on low flame, stirring occasionally, till almost done. Add 1 cup water and poppy seed paste. Cook till dry and tender. Serves 6–8.

Zucchini Treat

2 cups zucchini, sliced

1 medium eggplant, diced
2 medium tomatoes,
blanched and sliced
4 cups milk
½ teaspoon black pepper powder
1 green chili, finely chopped
3 tablespoons ghee
1 teaspoon cumin seeds
½ teaspoon mustard seeds
½ teaspoon turmeric powder
1 teaspoon coriander powder
½ teaspoon garam masala
salt to taste

In saucepan, bring milk to boil. Add lemon juice or citric acid to curdle. Pour into muslin cloth. Wash with cold water. Let hang for 1 hour; crumble. In skillet, heat ghee. Add mustard seeds and cumin seeds. When popping stops, add eggplants, chilis, turmeric, and salt and mix well. Fry for 2–3 minutes. Add zucchini and 1 cup water. Mix well. Cover and cook on low flame till almost done. Add remaining ingredients and ½ cup water. Cook till soft. Serves 6–8.

Savories

Kachori

Kachoris are one of the nicest savories when served with a chutney. Unlike *samosas, kachoris* are very thin and crisp. They are also very nice when served with a sour cream dip as an appetizer.

> DOUGH:
> *2½ cups all-purpose white flour*
> *1 tablespoon ghee*
> *ghee for deep frying*
> *salt to taste*

Mix together flour and salt. Rub in ghee, mixing till lumpy. Add enough yogurt to form a soft dough. Take a 2-inch ball and form it into a cup, filling with your favorite filling. Gather up edges and press in hand delicately to form a small cutlet or round flat *kachori*. Heat enough ghee for deep frying till smoking. Then reduce heat to low. Put *kachoris* in upside down, turning occasionally to brown both sides. When light brown, remove and drain. Serve with a savory chutney. Makes 16 *kachoris*.

> PEA FILLING:
> *2 cups peas, boiled and mashed*
> *1 cup milk*
> *1 green chili, finely chopped*
> *½-inch piece ginger root, grated*
> *3 tablespoons ghee*

½ teaspoon cinnamon powder
1 teaspoon turbinado sugar
pinch of asafetida
1 teaspoon garam masala
1 teaspoon cumin powder
1 teaspoon coriander leaves
salt to taste

In frying pan, heat ghee. Add chili, ginger, and asafetida and fry till brown. Add all ingredients and mix well. Cook till dry.

POTATO FILLING:
2 cups potatoes, boiled and mashed
½ cup peas, boiled
2 green chilis, finely chopped
½ teaspoon black pepper powder
3 tablespoons ghee
1 teaspoon cumin powder
1 teaspoon coriander powder
1 teaspoon garam masala
1 teaspoon lime juice
salt to taste

In frying pan, heat ghee. Add chilis and ginger and fry briefly. Add potatoes and peas and mix well. Fry for 5 minutes. Add all other ingredients. Mix in well and remove from flame.

URAD DAL FILLING #1:
1 cup urad dal
2 tablespoons ghee
1 teaspoon chili powder
¼ teaspoon asafetida
salt to taste

Soak *dal* overnight. Grind into paste. In frying pan, heat ghee. Add chilis and asafetida and fry briefly. Add *dal* and salt. Cook a few minutes.

URAD DAL FILLING #2:
1 cup urad dal
3 tablespoons ghee
1 teaspoon black pepper powder
½ teaspoon coriander powder
½ teaspoon cumin powder
½ teaspoon garam masala
salt to taste

Soak *dal* overnight and grind coarsely. In frying pan, heat ghee. Add *dal* and all spices and mix well. Fry 2–3 minutes, stirring constantly.

Samosa

A *samosa* is similar to a vegetable pie, except that it is deep-fried. It is best served hot with a chutney.

DOUGH:
2 cups all-purpose flour
1 cup sour yogurt
1 tablespoon ghee
½ teaspoon salt

Rub ghee into flour. Add salt and yogurt. Knead into a moist, firm dough. If the dough is not moist and firm, add yogurt, 1 table-spoon at a time, till it is the desired consistency. Pinch off 2-inch balls of dough. Place on greased surface. Roll each ball into a round 4–5 inches in diameter.

There are two ways to make a *samosa:*

1. Put 1 tablespoon of filling in the center of the *samosa* round. Rub the edges of the round with water. Fold over to make a half moon. Press the edges firmly together and twist them all around. Makes 12 *samosas.*

2. Cut the *samosa* round in half. Rub the edges with warm water. Fold and press seam till firm, forming a cone. Add filling. Press top firmly and twist. Makes 24 *samosas.*

Now you have your *samosas.* You can either fry them immediately, or you can cool the *samosas,* which also makes them crispy. Heat enough ghee or vegetable oil for deep frying. When the ghee or oil starts to get hot, add *samosas* and cook slowly, turning occasionally till golden brown. Drain and serve with a savory chutney.

CAULIFLOWER & PEAS FILLING:
1 medium cauliflower, grated
1 cup green peas, boiled
½ cup cream or milk
2 green chilis, finely chopped
1-inch piece ginger root, grated
4 tablespoons ghee
10 peppercorns, coarsely ground
½ teaspoon cinnamon powder
1 teaspoon cumin powder
1 teaspoon coriander powder
1 teaspoon garam masala
⅛ teaspoon asafetida
salt to taste

In frying pan, heat ghee. Add asafetida. When color changes, add peppercorns, chili, and ginger and mix well. When brown, add cauliflower and mix well. Fry 2–3 minutes, stirring constantly. Mix in cream or milk. Cover and cook on low flame till soft. Add peas, cumin, coriander, and salt. Cook till dry, stirring constantly. Add *garam masala* and mash a little.

FIVE VEGETABLES FILLING:
1 medium carrot, grated
1 small cauliflower, grated
1 medium beet, grated
1 small potato, peeled and grated
1 cup peas, boiled
2 green chilis, finely chopped
1-inch piece ginger root, grated
2 bay leaves, crushed
4 tablespoons ghee
1 teaspoon mustard seeds, crushed
⅛ teaspoon asafetida
1 teaspoon cumin powder
1 teaspoon coriander powder
1 tablespoon garam masala
1 tablespoon turbanaro sugar
½ teaspoon black pepper powder
salt to taste

In skillet, heat ghee. Add bay leaves and asafetida. When color changes, add chili and ginger and mix well. Fry briefly. Add all vegetables, salt, and ½ cup water. Mix well. Cover and cook on low flame till soft, stirring occasionally. Add *garam masala*, coriander, and sugar. Cook till dry, then mash.

FANCY POTATO FILLING:
3 medium potatoes, peeled
ghee for deep frying
½ cup raisins

¼ cup cashews
1 tablespoon turbinado sugar
1 teaspoon cumin powder
½ teaspoon red chili powder
2 teaspoon coriander powder
½ teaspoon turmeric powder
1 teaspoon garam masala
handful of coriander leaves
salt to taste
½ cup cream (optional)

Slice potatoes into fingers and deep-fry till brown. Drain and cool. In mixing bowl, combine all ingredients with potatoes, mashing together.

Pakora

Pakoras are simply vegetables, battered and deep-fried. They are excellent served hot as a side dish with a chutney.

POTATO PAKORA:
2 medium potatoes,
    peeled diced and boiled
2 cup chickpea flour
ghee for deep frying
1 green chilis, finely chopped
1 inch piece ginger root, grated
1 teaspoon coriander powder
1 teaspoon cumin powder
1 teaspoon garam masala
1 teaspoon powdered black pepper
handful of coriander leaves
salt to taste

Mash potatoes. In mixing bowl, combine chili, ginger, coriander leaves, pepper, and salt. Roll into 1-inch balls; set aside. Mix all other spices with chickpea flour, adding enough water to make a nice batter. Heat enough ghee for deep frying. When ghee starts smoking, lower heat. Dip balls in batter, covering completely. Deep-fry till golden brown. Drain and serve with chutney. (Many consider tamarind chutney the best.) Serves 6–8.

CAULIFLOWER PAKORA:
1 large cauliflower, cut into flowerets
ghee for deep frying
2 cups chickpea flour
1 cup yogurt, beaten
⅛ teaspoon asafetida
1 inch piece ginger root, grated
1 tablespoon cumin powder
1 teaspoon garam masala
1 teaspoon turmeric powder
1 teaspoon coriander powder
1 teaspoon black pepper powder
salt to taste

Blanch cauliflower; drain. Mix all spices with flour. Mix in yogurt and enough water to form a nice batter. Heat ghee for deep frying. When ghee starts smoking, reduce heat. Dip cauliflower flowerets in batter. Deep-fry till golden brown, turning occasionally. Drain and serve with your favorite chutney. Serves 6–8.

ALL-PURPOSE BATTER:
2 cups garam flour
1 cup yogurt, beaten
½ teaspoon chili powder
1 teaspoon cumin powder
½ teaspoon cinnamon powder

1 teaspoon garam masala
1 tablespoon sesame seeds
1 teaspoon black pepper powder
salt to taste

Mix all spices with flour. Add yogurt and enough water to form a nice batter. Serves 6–8.

VEGETABLES TO USE:
1. Zucchini sliced lengthwise
     or cut in rounds
2. Whole cherry tomatoes
3. Chilis cut in quarters
4. Peppers cut in strips
5. Sliced eggplant

Hot & Sweet Chutneys

So hot you can't eat them, so sweet you can't resist—these chutneys are excellent dishes to start the taste buds going.

Fig Chutney

2 cups dried figs
1 tablespoon ghee
½ teaspoon cumin seeds
1 green chili, finely chopped
½ cup turbinado sugar
juice of 1 lime
¼ teaspoon cardamon powder

In saucepan, bring figs to boil in 2 cups water. Lower heat to medium, cook till soft, mash, and set aside. In frying pan, heat 1 tablespoon ghee. Add cumin seeds and chilis. When brown, add figs, sugar, and cardamon powder and mix well. Cook till thick. Add lime juice. Serve cold. Makes 2 cups.

Date Chutney

2 cups chopped dates
½ teaspoon cardamon powder
½ teaspoon cinnamon powder
¼ teaspoon chili powder
½ cup turbinado sugar

In saucepan, bring dates to boil in 2 cups water. Lower heat to medium and cook till soft; mash. Add all other ingredients, mix well, and cook 3–5 minutes. Serve cold. Makes 2 cups.

Raisin Chutney

1 cup raisins
2 green chilies
1-inch piece ginger root
juice of 1 lime
1 teaspoon cumin seeds, dry-roasted
salt to taste

Grind all ingredients in a food processor or blender. Makes 1 cup.

Plum Chutney

2 cups fresh purple plums, pitted
1 cup grated coconut
1 teaspoon cardamon powder
juice of 1 lime
1 cup turbinado sugar
1 tablespoon rose water

In saucepan, bring to boil 1 cup water. Add plums and steam till soft; mash. Add all ingredients and mix well. Cook on low flame till thick. Makes 3 cups.

Mango Chutney

1½ cups grated green mangoes
1 cup turbinado sugar

½ teaspoon cumin seeds
1-inch cinnamon stick
8 peppercorns
2 cloves
pinch of asafetida
⅛ teaspoon red chili powder

In mixing bowl, combine mangoes, sugar, and salt. Put all spices in a muslin cloth and tie tightly. In saucepan, mix mangoes with 1½ cups water, add muslin cloth of spices, and bring to a boil. Lower heat to simmer and cook till thick. Remove muslin cloth. Serve cool. Makes 2½ cups.

Apple Chutney #1

8 medium apples
1 tablespoon butter
2-inch piece ginger root, grated
1 cup turbinado sugar
pinch of asafetida
2 tablespoons salt
1 tablespoon chili powder

Peel, core, and slice apples into small pieces. In saucepan, bring apples, water, ginger, asafetida, chili powder, and salt to a boil, then lower heat. When apples are soft, add sugar and cook till thick. Makes 2½ cups.

Apple Chutney #2

8 medium apples
1 cup turbinado sugar
2 tablespoons ghee

1 teaspoon cumin seeds
2 green chilis, finely chopped
1-inch piece of ginger root, grated
1 teaspoon cinnamon powder
½ teaspoon nutmeg powder
1 teaspoon coriander powder
½ teaspoon salt

Peel, core, and slice apples into eighths. In saucepan, bring apples and 2 cups water to boil, then lower heat. When soft, add salt and sugar and mix well. In frying pan, heat ghee. Add cumin seeds, chilis, and ginger, mix well, and fry briefly. Add to apples with remaining spices. Mix well. Cook till thick. Makes 2½ cups.

Apricot Chutney

2 cups dried apricots, pitted
1 tablespoon ghee
¼ teaspoon cumin seeds
1 green chili, finely chopped
½ cup turbinado sugar
¼ teaspoon cinnamon powder
¼ teaspoon cardamon powder

In saucepan, bring apricots and 2 cups water to boil. When soft, mash into paste. In medium frying pan, heat ghee. Add cumin seeds and chilis and mix well. When brown, add apricots, cardamon, cinnamon, and sugar. Mix well. Cook till thick. Makes 2 cups.

Peanut Chutney

1 cup dry-roasted peanuts

1-inch piece ginger root
juice of 1 lime
1 teaspoon dry-roasted cumin seedss
salt to taste

Grind all ingredients to a paste with a mortar and pestle. Makes 1 cup.

Rhubarb Chutney

4 cups rhubarb, cut into small pieces
½ cup turbinado sugar
1-inch piece ginger root, grated
¼ teaspoon chili powder
2 tablespoons powdered almonds
pinch of asafetida

In saucepan, bring 2 cups water to boil. Add rhubarb and all ingredients. Mix well. Cook on low flame till soft and pulpy. Makes 4 cups.

Pineapple Chutney

1 large pineapple, peeled and diced
1 cup turbinado sugar
2 green chilis, finely chopped
1-inch piece ginger root, grated
1-inch piece of cinnamon stick, broken
3 tablespoons ghee
¼ teaspoon cardamon powder
½ teaspoon nutmeg powder
1 teaspoon cumin seeds
½ cup raisins
½ teaspoon coriander powder

In skillet, heat ghee. Add cumin seeds. When brown, add chilis, ginger, and cardamon and mix well. Fry briefly. Add pineapple. Mix well. Cover and cook on low flame till soft. Add remaining ingredients. Mash pineapple with a spoon. Cook 3–5 minutes. Makes 3 cups.

Green Papaya Chutney #1

1 large green papaya, peeled and
grated or cut into thin slices
1 cup turbinado sugar
1-inch piece ginger root, grated
¼ cup raisins
2 tablespoons ghee
½ teaspoon turmeric powder
1 teaspoon coriander powder
1 teaspoon cumin powder
2 green chilis, finely chopped
1 tablespoon anise seeds

In saucepan, heat ghee. Add anise seeds and chilis. Cook till light brown. Add papaya, mix well, and cook 8–10 minutes, stirring constantly. Add enough water to cover papaya by 1 inch. Then add all other ingredients except sugar. When papaya is soft, add sugar and mix well. Cook for 5 minutes. Makes 3½ cups.

Green Papaya Chutney #2

1 medium green papaya
juice of 2 lemons
1 cup turbinado sugar
¼ cup raisins

Peel skin off papaya. With potato peeler, slice papaya very thin (you should be able to see through the slices.) In saucepan, bring 4 cups water to boil, add papaya slices, cook 15–20 minutes, or till quite soft. Add sugar and more water if needed, 1 cup at a time. Cook 10–15 minutes. Add raisins and lemon juice. Reduce heat to simmer and cook 5–10 minutes, or till thick. Makes 3 cups.

Sesame Seed Chutney

¼ cup sesame seeds
1 tablespoon grated coconut
pinch of asafetida
1 teaspoon cumin seeds
2 red chilis, crushed
salt to taste

In frying pan, dry-roast separately the sesame seeds, coconut, chilis, and cumin seeds. Grind all ingredients into paste. Makes ¼ cup.

Cucumber Chutney

1 cup grated cucumber
¼ cup dry-roasted peanuts, ground
1 tablespoon coconut powder
½ teaspoon turbinado sugar
juice of 1 lime
2 tablespoons ghee
½ teaspoon cumin seeds
pinch of asafetida
handful of coriander leaves
salt to taste

In medium frying pan, heat ghee. Add cumin seeds and asafetida. When brown, add all ingredients except coriander leaves and mix well. Cook 3–5 minutes, stirring constantly. Garnish with coriander leaves. Makes 1¼ cups.

Potato Chutney

4 medium potatoes,
   sliced ⅛ inch thick
2 green chilis
1-inch piece ginger root
1 teaspoon coconut powder
1¼ teaspoon cumin seeds
pinch of asafetida
3 tablespoons ghee
1 teaspoon coriander seeds
½ teaspoon turmeric powder
¼ teaspoon mustard seeds
handful of coriander leaves
salt to taste

With a little water, grind into a paste the chilis, ginger, coconut, 1 teaspoon cumin seeds, and coriander seeds. Mix in salt and turmeric. Rub this paste on both sides of the potato slices. In frying pan, heat ghee. Add mustard seeds and rest of cumin seeds and mix well. When popping stops, add asafetida and fry briefly. Add potato slices. Cover and cook on low flame on both sides till soft. Garnish with coriander leaves. Makes 3½ cups.

Peach Chutney #1

6 cups sliced peaches
1½ cups turbinado sugar

2 green chilis, finely chopped
1-inch piece ginger root, grated
½ teaspoon cardamon powder
3 tablespoons ghee
1 teaspoon cumin seeds
2-inch cinnamon stick, crushed
½ teaspoon nutmeg
½ teaspoon chili powder

In saucepan, heat ghee. Add cumin seeds and cinnamon stick. When brown, add chilis and ginger and mix well. Fry briefly. Add peaches and 1 cup water. Cover and cook on low flame till soft. With potato masher, mash coarsely and add remaining ingredients. Stir and cook till thick. Makes 5½ cups.

Peach Chutney #2

5 cups of mashed peaches (blended)
1 cup brown sugar
juice of 1 lime
4 tablespoons ghee
¼ cup finely chopped almonds
½ cup raisins
½ teaspoon chili powder
½ teaspoon black pepper powder
1 teaspoon coriander powder
1 teaspoon cinnamon powder
½ teaspoon cardamon powder

In saucepan, heat ghee. Add almonds and fry till light brown. Add mashed peaches and mix well. Add all other ingredients and 1 cup water and mix well. Cover and cook on low flame till thick. Makes 5 cups.

Pear Chutney

4 cups diced pears
1 cup sugar
½ cup heavy cream
1 teaspoon cinnamon powder
½ teaspoon cardamon powder
½ teaspoon nutmeg powder
½ teaspoon chili powder

In saucepan, mix pears and 1 cup water. Cook on low flame till soft. Mash coarsely. Mix in remaining ingredients and cook on low flame till thick. Makes 4 cups.

Banana Chutney

2 cups sliced bananas
½ cup sugar
juice of 2 limes
3 tablespoons ghee
1 teaspoon cumin seeds
½ teaspoon cinnamon powder
½ teaspoon chili powder

In frying pan, heat ghee. Add cumin seeds. When brown, add bananas and mix well. Add remaining ingredients. When sugar is dissolved, remove from heat. Makes 2 cups.

Coriander Chutney

2 cups coriander leaves, chopped

1½ cups yogurt
1 tablespoon lemon juice
1 teaspoon coriander powder
1 teaspoon cumin powder
1 green chili
1-inch piece ginger root
½ teaspoon salt

Blend all ingredients. Makes 2 cups.

Tamarind Chutney

1½ cups fresh tamarind,
*   broken in small pieces*
1 teaspoon coriander powder
1 teaspoon cumin powder
¼ teaspoon chili powder
½ cup turbinado sugar
½ teaspoon salt

In saucepan, bring 2½ cups water and tamarind to boil. Stir and cook 10 minutes, then pour through strainer, pushing pulp with wooden spoon, and periodially scraping bottom of strainer. Continue till all pulp is through, and all that remains in strainer is seeds and fiber. Mix strained tamarind with all other ingredients and cook on medium flame till thick. Makes 2 cups.

Coconut Chutney

1½ cups grated coconut, fresh or dry
1 tablespoon coriander leaves
2 cups yogurt

1-inch piece ginger
2 green chilis
1 teaspoon cumin powder
1 teaspoon coriander powder
½ teaspoon salt
3 tablespoons ghee
⅛ teaspoon asafetida
1 tablespoon urad dal, split
1 teaspoon mustard seeds
a few curry leaves

Blend together coconut, yogurt, coriander powder, cumin powder, chilis, ginger, coriander leaves, and salt. In frying pan, heat ghee, then add mustard seeds. When popping stops, add asafetida, curry leaves, and *dal* and mix well. Cook till *dal* turns red. Pour into coconut and mix well. Makes 3½ cups.

Tomato Chutneys

The red tomato chutneys are good for french fries and *pakoras*. The green tomato chutneys are excellent just as they are.

Tomato Chutney #1

5 large tomatoes, peeled and blanched
1 cup turbinado sugar
1-inch piece ginger root, grated
2 green chilis, finely chopped
2 tablespoons ghee
⅛ teaspoon asafetida
1 teaspoon garam masala
½ teaspoon salt

In frying pan, heat ghee. Add chilis, ginger, and asafetida and mix well. When color changes, add tomatoes. Cook on low flame, stirring, for 5–10 minutes. Add sugar, salt, and *garam masala*. Cook till thick. Makes 5 cups.

Tomato Chutney #2

6 large tomatoes, peeled and blanched
2 green chilis, finely chopped
1-inch piece ginger root, grated
2 tablespoons ghee
⅛ teaspoon asafetida
2 bay leaves

½ teaspoon cardamon powder
1 cup turbinado sugar
salt to taste

In frying pan, heat ghee. Add chilis, ginger, bay leaves, and asafetida and mix well. Cook till brown. Add tomatoes, mix well, and cook on low flame 5–10 minutes. Mix in all other ingredients and cook till thick. Makes 6 cups.

Tomato Chutney #3

6 large tomatoes, peeled and blanched
2 cups turbinado sugar
handful of raisins
3 bay leaves
juice of 1 lime

Mix all ingredients except lime juice in saucepan. Cook on low flame till tomatoes become glossy and thick. Add lime juice, mix well. Serve cool. Makes 6 cups.

Tomato Chutney #4

8 large tomatoes, peeled and blanched
2 green chilis, finely chopped
1-inch piece ginger root, grated
6 whole cardamon pods,
     or ½ teaspoon cardamon powder
1-inch stick of cinnamon,
     or ½ teaspoon cinnamon powder
3 tablespoons ghee
½ teaspoon cumin seeds

½ teaspoon mustard seeds
4 peppercorns
2 bay leaves
⅛ teaspoon asafetida
1 cup turbinado sugar
handful of coriander leaves
salt to taste

In saucepan, heat ghee. Add cumin seeds, mustard seeds, chilis, ginger, bay leaves, and peppercorns and mix well. When popping stops, add tomatoes. Mix well and cook on low flame till tomatoes break down. Add cardamon, cinnamon, sugar, asafetida, and salt and mix well. Cook till thick. Garnish with coriander leaves. Makes 8 cups.

Green Tomato Chutney #1

6 large green tomatoes
¼ cup turbinado sugar
1 teaspoon cinnamon powder
½ teaspoon salt

In saucepan, bring to boil tomatoes, water, and salt. When skin of tomatoes begins to peel or crack, remove them from water and let cool. Peel tomatoes and mash into paste. Mix all ingredients in a skillet and cook on low flame 5–10 minutes. Makes 5½ cups.

Green Tomato Chutney #2

5 large green tomatoes
2 green chilis
3 teaspoons sesame seeds

2 tablespoons grated coconut
1 tablespoon ghee
¼ teaspoon cumin seeds
¼ teaspoon mustard seeds
pinch of asafetida
salt to taste

In frying pan, dry-roast sesame seeds. With a mortar and pestle, grind to paste sesame seeds, chilis, and coconut. Blend tomatoes. In skillet, heat ghee, and add cumin seeds, mustard seeds, and asafetida and mix well. When popping stops, add tomato and paste. Mix well. Add salt and cook for 5–10 minutes. Makes 5 cups.

Raita

Raita is a cold, spicy vegetable dish which is usually eaten at the end of a meal. It is similar to a dip, and is made with yogurt. (Sour cream can be used in place of yogurt, if desired.)

Eggplant Raita

1 large eggplant
1½ cups yogurt, beaten till smooth
1 green chili, finely chopped
1 teaspoon grated coconut
2 tablespoons ghee
½ teaspoon cumin seeds
pinch of asafetida
handful of coriander leaves
salt to taste

Roast eggplant over open fire till all skin turns color. Put in cold water and peel. In mixing bowl, mash into pulp with coconut, yogurt, and salt. In frying pan, heat ghee. Add cumin, asafetida, and chilis and mix well. When brown, add to eggplant mixture. Garnish with coriander leaves. Serves 3–4.

Cucumber Raita

1 large cucumber, peeled and grated
¼ cup peanuts, dry-roasted and pounded
1 tablespoon grated coconut
2 tablespoons ghee

½ teaspoon cumin seeds
pinch of asafetida
juice of 1 lime
handful of coriander leaves
salt to taste

In skillet, heat ghee. Add cumin seeds and asafetida. When brown, add all ingredients. Mix well. Cook 1–2 minutes. Garnish with coriander leaves. Serves 3–4.

Gujarati Vegetable Raita

2 cups yogurt, beaten till smooth
1 small carrot, grated
1 small tomato, diced
1 small cucumber, grated
1 small beet root, grated
2 green chilis, finely chopped
½ teaspoon ginger powder
1 teaspoon cumin seeds,
    dry-roasted and powdered
a few mint leaves
handful of coriander leaves
salt to taste

In mixing bowl, combine all ingredients together and garnish with beet root. Serves 5–6.

Gujarati Banana Raita

2 ripe bananas, peeled and sliced thin
2 cups yogurt, beaten till smooth
¼ teaspoon mustard powder

1-inch piece ginger root, grated
pinch of asafetida
a few mint leaves
handful of coriander leaves
salt to taste
red chili powder to taste

In mixing bowl, combine all ingredients except mint and coriander leaves. After mixing, garnish with greens. Serves 4–6.

Pumpkin Raita

1½ cups pumpkin,
    cut into 1-inch cubes
1 cup yogurt, beaten till smooth
2 green chilis, finely chopped
2 tablespoons ghee
½ teaspoon mustard seeds
pinch of asafetida
1 teaspoon turbinado sugar
handful of coriander leaves
salt to taste

In saucepan, put chilis, pumpkin, salt, and 1 cup water and mix well. Cover and cook on low flame till soft. In mixing bowl, mash into paste and stir in yogurt and sugar. In frying pan, heat ghee. Add mustard seeds and asafetida. When popping stops, add to mixture and mix well. Garnish with coriander leaves. Serves 3–4.

North Indian Cabbage Raita

1½ cups grated cabbage
1 cup yogurt

1 green chili, finely chopped
1-inch piece ginger root, grated
a few cashews, chopped
a few peanuts, chopped
a few raisins
2 tablespoons ghee
1 teaspoon cumin seeds
½ teaspoon mustard seeds
½ teaspoon garam masala
handful of coriander leaves
salt to taste

In mixing bowl, combine cabbage, yogurt, nuts, raisins, salt, and *garam masala*. In frying pan, heat ghee. Add cumin seeds and mustard seeds. When popping stops, add chilis and ginger, mix well, and fry briefly. Mix into cabbage mixture. Garnish with coriander leaves. Serves 3–4.

Chickpea Raita

ghee for deep frying
1 cup chickpea flour
2½ cups yogurt
1 teaspoon cumin powder
⅛ teaspoon cayenne powder
1 tablespoon coriander leaves,
*   finely chopped*
1 teaspoon salt

In mixing bowl, combine chickpea flour, ½ teaspoon salt, and ¼ cup water. Mix till batter is formed. In wok, heat ghee. Put 1 drop of batter in ghee. If it floats to top, ghee is the proper temperature. In collander or pan with ⅛-inch holes, pour 2 tablespoons batter, and with spatula, press through holes into ghee till surface of ghee is covered. Fry till crisp. Remove and repeat till all batter is used. In mixing bowl, combine yogurt, cumin powder, salt, and cayenne and mix well. Stir in chickpea balls till evenly distributed. Garnish with coriander leaves and let soak 15 minutes before serving. Serves 4–6.

Pickles

Pickles add a nice accent to your favorite meal, and usually one tablespoonful is all that is required. The most important things to remember when preparing pickles is that they should always be stored in sterilized glass jars, and you should never touch the pickles with your fingers once they are in the jar—as soon as germs enter the jar, mold will spoil the pickles. Always keep the cover tight while letting your pickles age in the sun. Stir with a wooden spoon once a day only, unless the recipe calls for more. Store the jars in clean surroundings. To sterilize your jars, bring water to a boil and submerge them for 5–10 minutes. Remove and dry them with a clean cloth. Then put in the mixture, cover, and place in the sun.

Mango Pickle #1

10 green mangoes
¼ cup chili powder
1 tablespoon mustard powder
½ teaspoon asafetida
1½ tablespoons fenugreek powder
2 cups sesame oil
1½ cups salt

Remove pit and cut mangoes into 2-inch pieces. In a small pan, mix all spices. Add sesame oil little by little, mixing well. When all oil is added and well mixed, stir in mangoes. Transfer to sterilized glass jars and place in sun for 6 weeks, stirring once a day with wooden spoon. Makes 2 quarts.

Mango Pickle #2

8 green mangoes
2 tablespoons turmeric powder
2 tablespoons chili powder
½ cup salt
1 teaspoon asafetida
½ cup mustard seeds, powdered
½ cup fenugreek seeds, powdered
2 cups peanut oil

Remove pit and cut mangoes into 2-inch pieces. In a small pan, mix all spices. Add peanut oil little by little, mixing well. When all oil is added and well mixed, stir in mangoes. Transfer to sterilized glass jars and place in sun for 6 weeks, stirring once a day with wooden spoon. Makes 2 quarts.

Sweet Mango Pickle #1

8 green mangoes
½ cup salt
1 tablespoon fenugreek seeds
½ cup chili powder
½ teaspoon asafetida
1 teaspoon coriander powder
2 cups brown sugar
2 cups sesame oil

Remove pits and cut mangoes into 2-inch pieces. Mix with salt and leave for 3 days. Then put mango pieces in sun to dry for 6–8 hours. In saucepan, heat oil, then add fenugreek. When fenugreek turns brown, add mustard powder and asafetida. Stir and remove from heat. Add remaining spices and mangoes and mix well. Transfer to sterilized glass jar and let set, stirring once a day for 15 days. Then add brown sugar. Mix well and let set 15 more days. Anytime from this point you can serve. Makes 2 quarts.

Sweet Mango Pickle #2

20 green mangoes
6 cups brown sugar
½ cup salt
20 dried chilis
1 cup coriander powder
1 cup chili powder
1 cup mustard powder
½ cup fenugreek seeds, split
1 teaspoon asafetida
1 teaspoon cinnamon powder
2 cups sesame oil

Remove pits and cut mangoes into 1-inch pieces. Mix with salt and let set for 2 days. Dry mango pieces in shade for 1 day. In saucepan, heat oil. Add red chilis. When color changes, add all other spices. Cook briefly, then remove from heat. When cool, mix in mangoes. Store in sterilized jars. After 10 days, add sugar and mix well. Let set for 2 weeks, stirring every day. Makes 1 gallon.

Grated Mango Pickle

8 green mangoes
3 cups brown sugar
½ cup salt
½ cup chili powder
1 teaspoon cardamon powder

Grate mango. Mix in salt. Let set for 4–5 hours. Squeeze out juice. In skillet, mix all other ingredients and cook on medium flame till syrupy. Transfer to sterilized glass jar. This can be served the next day. Makes 2 quarts.

Lime Pickle #1

3 dozen limes
1 tablespoon chili powder
10 green chilis, crushed to paste
1 tablespoon fenugreek powder
1 teaspoon mustard powder
1 cup salt

Wash limes and cut each into 4 pieces. In saucepan, mix with all ingredients. Cook on low flame till limes turn reddish. Store in sterilized glass jar for 2 months. Stir occasionally. Makes 1 gallon.

Lime Pickle #2

2 dozen limes
½ cup salt
2 tablespoons turmeric powder
2 cups red chilis
½ teaspoon asafetida powder
2 teaspoon mustard seeds
2-inch piece of ginger root, grated
½ cup sesame oil

Wash limes and cut each into 4 pieces. Mix with salt and turmeric and store in sterilized jar for 6–7days. Grind chilis into paste with juice of 1 lime. In frying pan, heat oil. Add mustard seeds and asafetida. When popping stops, add all other ingredients and mix well. Cool and mix into limes. Store in sun for 2 months. Makes 3½ quarts.

Lime Pickle #3

3 dozen limes
10 green chilis, finely chopped
1 pound beans (any variety)
½ cup salt
½ cup turmeric powder
½ cup finely-chopped ginger root

Wash limes and cut each into 4 pieces. Mix with salt and turmeric and store in sterilized jar for 4 days. Add chilis, beans, and ginger and mix well. Store for 1 month. Makes 1 gallon.

Lime Pickle #4

3 dozen limes
1 cup chili powder
½ teaspoon black pepper powder
¼ teaspoon ajwan seeds, or oregano
1 teaspoon cumin powder
2 pinches of asafetida
2 tablespoons turmeric powder
1 cup salt
1 tablespoon mustard powder
5 cloves, powdered
½-inch piece of cinnamon stick,
*   powdered*
2 cups sesame oil

Wash limes and cut each into 4 pieces. Extract juice from 10 limes. Mix juice with all spices and limes, including 10 squeezed limes. Add oil and mix well. Put in sterilized glass jar and place in sun for 3–4 weeks, stirring every day. Makes 1 gallon.

Carrot Pickle

2 pounds carrots
2 tablespoons mustard seeds
1 tablespoon fenugreek seeds
1 teaspoon cumin seeds
1 teaspoon turmeric powder
1½ cups safflower oil
2 tablespoon red chili powder
2 tablespoons turbinado sugar
3 cloves, powdered
1 teaspoon cinnamon powder
1 teaspoon salt

Peel carrots and cut into thin 3-inch pieces. In frying pan, heat 2 tablespoons oil. Add mustard seeds, fenugreek seeds, and cumin seeds. When popping stops, remove from heat and grind. Mix in all spices. Mix with carrots. Add oil. Mix again and put in sterilized jar. Set aside for 1 week. Makes 2 quarts.

Turnip Pickle

2 pounds turnips
¼ cup mustard powder
½ cup salt
½ cup chili powder

Wash and peel turnips. Cut into ¼-inch pieces. Put in saucepan. Cover with water and boil for 2 minutes. Remove from heat. When cool, drain and add all spices and mix well. Store in sterilized glass jar and put in sun for 10 days. When pickle becomes sour, it's ready (about 2 weeks). Makes 2 quarts.

Potato Pickle

12 medium potatoes
½ cup mustard powder
1 cup salt
1½ cups turmeric powder
1 cup sesame oil

In saucepan, boil potatoes. Peel and cut into pieces. In skillet, heat oil. Add mustard powder. Remove from flame. Add salt, turmeric, and potatoes. Mix well. Store in sterilized glass jar for 1 week. Makes 1 gallon.

Eggplant Pickle

15 small eggplants (3–4 inches)
3 tablespoons mustard powder
3 tablespoons chili powder
1 teaspoon turmeric powder
½ cup salt
¼ cup sesame oil

Wash and dry eggplants. Cut into quarters, halfway through. In saucepan, cook eggplant in boiling salted water till soft. Drain and cool. Mix in all spices with oil. Stuff into eggplants. Transfer to sterilized glass jar. Cover with water, gently shaking every day. Place in sun for 1 day. In 5 days pickle is ready. Makes 1½ quarts.

Cauliflower Pickle

1 large cauliflower
1½ cups sesame oil
1 tablespoon turmeric powder
1 tablespoon mustard seeds
juice of 1 lime
1 teaspoon chili powder
salt to taste

Wash cauliflower and cut into small pieces. In saucepan, bring to boil 8 cups of water. Add cauliflower and blanch for 1 minute. Mix in turmeric, salt, and chili powder and mix well. In frying pan, heat oil, then add mustard seeds. When popping stops, add to cauliflower with lime juice and mix well. Serve in 6 hours. Lasts for 3 days. Makes 2 quarts.

Sweet Potato Pickle

12 medium sweet potatoes
4 cups mustard oil, or safflower oil
¼ cup salt
½ cup mustard powder
¼ cup chili powder
¼ teaspoon asafetida
¼ cup grated ginger
1 tablespoon garam masala
1 tablespoon cumin powder
½ teaspoon turmeric powder

Peel potatoes and cut into ½-inch cubes. In wok, in small batches, deep-fry in 4 cups oil till light brown. Drain and cool oil. In saucepan, heat 2 tablespoons oil. Add ginger and asafetida and fry briefly. Add all other spices. Mix well. Remove from heat. Mix in fried potatoes and cooled oil. Transfer to sterilized glass jar. Place in sun for 4–5 days, shaking every day. Makes 1 gallon.

Chili Pickle

2 pounds long green chilis
½ cup mustard powder
1 teaspoon asafetida
1 teaspoon turmeric powder
½ cup salt
1 cup peanut oil

Wash and dry chilis. Slit down middle halfway though. Remove seeds and stalk. In frying pan, heat oil. Add all spices and fry briefly. Cool and stuff into chilis. Transfer to sterilized glass jar and place in sun for 1 month, stirring or shaking once a day. Makes 1½–2 quarts.

Flat Breads

Chapati

3 cups atta (chapati flour),
*   or sifted whole wheat flour*
¾ cup warm water
½ teaspoon salt
¼ cup melted butter or ghee

Mix together flour and salt. Add water slowly till dough is formed; knead for 5–6 minutes. Cover for 30 minutes. Place cast-iron griddle over medium flame. Knead dough again for a few minutes, then divide into 20 equal-size balls. Press each ball between palms, then roll on floured board into thin, round shapes. Pat excess flour off, then place on hot griddle. When *chapati* starts to bubble, turn with metal tongs. When second side starts to bubble, transfer to open gas flame. Cook until it begins to puff, then turn over. When completely puffed, remove from flame. (Small brown spots are a good sign, indicating that the *chapati* is properly cooked.) Brush with melted butter or ghee and transfer each *chapati* to a bowl in an even stack. Keep bowl covered to retain heat. Best served hot. Makes 20 *chapatis*.

Puri

3 cups atta (chapati flour), or 2 cups sifted whole wheat
flour and 1 cup unbleached white flour

1 tablespoon melted ghee
¾ cup warm water
½ teaspoon salt
ghee for deep frying

In mixing bowl, combine flour and salt. Rub in ghee. Slowly add water, mixing till dough is formed. Knead for 5–6 minutes. Cover and let sit for 30 minutes. Knead again for a few minutes, then divide dough into 15 balls, flattening each with palm. Grease rolling surface and rolling pin with ghee. Roll out each *puri* by guiding dough in one direction, then turning and rolling again into disk shape. Heat ghee till it begins to smoke. Lower heat to medium, wait a few minutes, then add a *puri*. It will sink to the bottom for a few seconds, then rise. With a slotted spoon, dunk *puri* till it starts to puff, then flip on other side for a few seconds. Remove and place in colander to drain. Best served hot. Makes 15 *puris*.

Paratha

3 cups atta (chapati flour), or 2 cups
sifted whole wheat flour
and 1 cup unbleached white flour
¼ cup melted ghee
⅔ cup warm water
⅔ teaspoon salt

In mixing bowl, combine flour and salt. Rub in ghee. Add water slowly till dough is formed. Knead for 5–6 minutes. Cover and let sit for 30 minutes. Knead again for a few minutes, then divide dough into 12 balls, flattening each with palm into a thick disk. Spread a little ghee over disk and fold in half. Spread ghee on half disk and fold again into triangle. Grease rolling surface and rolling pin. Roll out triangle to large, thin *paratha*. Heat large cast-iron griddle on medium flame. Place *paratha* on griddle and move around till it begins to puff, then turn over, spread with ghee, and wait till it completely puffs. Turn and brush ghee on other side. When both sides are showing brown spots, *paratha* is done. Best served hot with a favorite chutney or vegetable dish. Makes 12 *parathas.*

Sweets

Laddu

4½ cups besan (chickpea) flour
3 tablespoons finely chopped walnuts
1½ cups unsalted butter
¾ teaspoon ground cardamon seeds
2 cups powdered sugar

In a thick-bottomed frying pan or wok, melt butter on low flame. Mix in flour, stirring constantly until toasted (about 15 minutes). Mix in nuts and cardamon, cooking for a few minutes. Remove from flame and add powdered sugar. Mix well and pour into cake pan. Let cool, then cut into 48 small squares.

Luglu

1½ cups sugar
1 cup chopped dried figs
1 cup chopped dried apricots
1 cup pitted dates (halved)
1 cup finely chopped almonds
    or cashews
½ cup finely chopped pistacios
½ cup raisins
1 cup grated coconut
½ teaspoon ground nutmeg
¼ teaspoon ground cloves

1½ cups besan (chickpea) flour
ghee for deep-frying

In large saucepan, place 2 cups water, sugar, spices, and dried fruit. Bring to boil, then lower flame to medium and cook, stirring constantly till mixture becomes a thick sauce (dried fruit should retain chunkiness and not completely liquify). Reduce heat to simmer. Heat ghee in wok on medium flame. In large mixing bowl, mix flour and ¾ cup water to form a thick batter. Hold a spoon or colander with large holes over the ghee and pour batter, using rubber spatula to force through holes. Fill the wok with droplets (*bundis*), just enough to cover surface. With slotted spoon, move *bundis* around till they turn crispy, not brown (3–4 minutes). Remove and place in colander. Continue cooking, using all batter. When finished, add *bundis,* coconut, and nuts to dried-fruit sauce and mix well. Remove from flame and let cool for a few minutes. With moistened hands, form balls to desired size, and place on tray to harden. Makes 40–50 *luglus.*

Gulabjamun

1 cup unbleached white flour
6 cups powdered milk
2 teaspoons baking soda
1½ teaspoons ground cardomon pod
1 teaspoon whole cardamon pod
1½ cups whipping cream
12 cups sugar
½ teaspoon saffron
clean ghee for deep-frying

In large saucepan, place sugar and 12 cups water. Bring to boil and add saffron and cardamon pods. Boil 5–10 minutes, then set aside. (3 tablespoons of rose water can be added instead of saffron and cardamon, if preferred.) In large mixing bowl, combine powdered milk, flour, baking soda, and ground cardamon. Mix well. Make a space in the middle and slowly add whipping cream, mixing to make a firm dough. Form dough into 1-inch balls. Roll each ball in circular motion between palms, increasing pressure till smooth and there are no cracks. As each ball is rolled, transfer to tray. Heat ghee in wok on very low flame. Carefully place balls into ghee. They will sink to bottom. With slotted spoon, gently stir them as they rise again to the surface. Increase flame slightly, and with the back of the spoon, spin the balls as they slowly swell and cook evenly to a rich golden brown. When done, remove from ghee and place in warm syrup to soak (at least 4 hours), then test—they should be soft and spongy. If necessary, continue soaking till preferred consistency is reached. Serve warm. Makes 60–70 *gulabjamuns*.

Burfi

6 cups whipping cream
3 cups whole milk
½ cup sugar

Pour whipping cream and milk into wide, heavy-bottomed stainless steel pot. Place on high flame, stirring occasionally, till milk begins to boil. Lower flame, bringing milk to slow boil. Stir occasionally with wide steel spatula. As milk thickens, stir vigorously to prevent scorching. When *burfi* becomes pastelike, add sugar and mix well. Constant stirring is required at this point, as well as periodic scraping of the side of the pot. Continue cooking till *burfi* becomes thick and sticky, then stir for a few more minutes. Scrape *burfi* onto buttered plate. When cool, form into a square cake 1-inch thick. Cut into 60–70 1-inch pieces.

Saffron Sweet Rice

8 cups milk
½ cup white rice
¾ cup sugar
1 tablespoon saffron strings
1 teaspoon cardamon powder
½ cup finely chopped pistacios
1 cup whipping cream

In saucepan, combine milk, sugar, rice, and saffron. Bring to boil, stirring occasionally. When it starts to foam, lower flame to low boil, and cook for 1 hour while continuing to stir (after 50 minutes, add cardamon powder). When finished, add chopped pistacio. Put in stainless steel container and refrigerate for 8 hours. Then mix in cream and stir well. Serve cold. Serves 4–6.

VARIATION: Instead of saffron and pistacio, add 2 cups sliced strawberries.

Sandesh

16 cups whole milk
7 tablespoons lemon juice
¾ cup sugar
1½ teaspoons cardamon powder
*   or few pinches saffron (optional)*
coconut powder (optional)

Bring milk to boil, stirring occasionally. When foam starts to rise, add lemon juice and stir till curds form. Turn off flame and let sit for a few minutes. Wrap curd in cheese cloth, rinse a few seconds under running water, then squeeze out liquid. Place wrapped curd under weight and press for 10–15 minutes. Remove curd from cloth and place on clean, dry surface. Knead vigorously till curd is soft and free of lumps, then divide in half. Knead sugar into half of curd for a few minutes, then place in frying pan on very low flame. Cook for about 5 minutes, stirring constantly with wooden spoon, till curd becomes runny, then thickens. Remove from pan and let cool for 10 minutes. Knead all curd together vigorously with heels of hands. (Cardamon or saffron can be added near the end of kneading.) Break off 2-inch pieces and form into oblong shapes, or use *sandesh* molds to form. Sprinkle with coconut. Makes 1½ pounds.

Halava

2 cups farina
4¼ cups water or milk
2¼ cups sugar
1 cup butter
¼ cup raisins
1 tablespoon cardamon
   powder

Put water or milk, sugar, raisins, and cardamon in saucepan. Mix well and place on medium flame. In another saucepan on medium flame, melt butter and mix in farina. When butter is absorbed, turn flame to low and cook, stirring occasionally till grains are light brown. When liquid comes to boil, slowly add to farina, stirring constantly to avoid lumps. Continue stirring till farina thickens and begins to leave sides of pan. Remove from flame. Serve warm. Serves 12–14.

VARIATION: 1 cup blueberries or sliced strawberries can be used instead of raisins and cardamon. Add after all water has been absorbed by farina.

Carrot Halava

5 cups shredded carrots
3 cups milk
1½ cups sugar
1 cup butter
½ cup raisins
½ cup blanched slivered
almonds or cashews
1 tablespoon cardamon
powder

Melt butter in saucepan on medium flame. Add carrots and mix well. Cover and let steam 5 minutes, stirring occasionally. Add milk and sugar, mix well, and bring to boil. Lower to slow boil and cook, stirring occasionally till carrots are soft and begin to break apart. Add nuts, raisins, and cardamon. Mix well and cook till thick (about 3–5 minutes). Serves 12–14.

Appendix:
Offering Food to Krishna

This cookbook is especially meant for spiritual vegetarians, who recognize that the food they eat is a gift from God (Krishna) and naturally feel inclined to show their appreciation and gratitude.

According to the *Bhagavad-gita,* the most famous of India's timeless books of spiritual wisdom, the best way to show your appreciation and gratitude is to offer your food to God before eating it yourself.

The *Gita* advises we see ourselves as servants in the house of God. And as good servants, it is our duty, and pleasure, to allow Him to enjoy the food we cook before we enjoy it.

By doing this, we can awaken our loving feelings for God. The tendency to love God is a natural impulse of the soul, and it can be brought out by such activities as cooking delicious vegetarian food for the pleasure of the Lord.

The most essential ingredient in any offering to Krishna is the love and devotion with which it is prepared.

One element of this love and devotion with respect to food is not offering anything to Krishna that would be displeasing to Him. Meat, fish, eggs, alcohol, onions, and garlic should not be offered to Krishna. One should therefore study labels on prepared foods to make sure they don't contain any of these things.

It is best that offerings to Krishna be displayed on special plates and cups are that are not used for any other purpose. Stainless steel plates and cups are preferred. They are obtainable from Hare Krishna temple gift stores, Indian specialty food stores, or online.

You may also want to set aside a special area in your home for making offerings to Krishna. This can take the form of a small altar, which could simply be a special shelf in a bookcase, or a table top.

On your altar you should place pictures of your spiritual master, Lord Krishna, and Lord Chaitanya (also obtainable from temple gift stores, or online from various websites such as Krishna. com).

According to the *Gita,* there is one God, who is known by many names in different parts of the world. Krishna is one of these names of God in the Sanskrit language. It refers to the personal aspect of God and means "all-attractive."

From time to time Krishna comes to this world, sometimes in His original form, and sometimes in other forms. Krishna Himself last appeared about 5,000 years ago, but a little over 500 years ago, He returned again to this world as Lord Chaitanya.

The present Hare Krishna movement, founded by His Divine Grace A. C. Bhaktivedanta Swami Prabhupada, comes in a direct line from Lord Chaitanya, who requested His followers to spread love of Krishna to every town and village in the world.

If you are seriously interested in learning the science of love of God, you will someday want to connect yourself with a living spiritual master through initiation. In that case, you would use a picture of your personal spiritual master for offering food. But till that time you may make offerings using a picture of Srila Prabhupada along with the pictures of Lord Krishna and Lord Chaitanya.

The very simplest kind of offering you can make is to place the offering before the pictures of Srila Prabhupada, Lord Krishna, and Lord Chaitanya and ask them to please accept it.

But the usual procedure is to say some traditional Sanskrit prayers, or mantras, which you will find below. Repeat each one softly three times. You do not have to repeat the English translations, but I have given them so you will know what the Sanskrit words of the mantras mean.

1) *nama om vishnu-padaya krsna-presthaya bhutale*
   srimate bhaktivedanta-svamin iti namine

   I offer my respectful obeisances unto His Divine Grace
   A. C. Bhaktivedanta Swami Prabhupada, who is very dear
   to Lord Krishna, having taken shelter at His lotus feet.

2) *namas te sarasvate devam gaura-vani-pracharine*
   nirvishesha-shunyavadi-paschatya-desha tarine

   Our respectful obeisances unto you, O spiritual master,
   servant of Sarasvati Goswami. You are kindly preaching the
   message of Lord Chaitanya and delivering the Western coun-
   tries, which are filled with impersonalism and voidism.

3) *namo maha-vadanyaya krishna-prema-pradaya te*
   krishnaya krishna-chaitanya-namne gaura-tvishe namaha

   I offer my respectful obeisances unto the Supreme Lord Sri
   Krishna Chaitanya, who is more magnanimous than any
   other incarnation, even Krishna Himself, because He is be-
   stowing freely what no one else has ever given—pure love
   of Krishna.

4) *namo-brahmanya-devaya go brahmana hitaya cha*
   jagadd-hitaya krishnaya govindaya namo namaha

   I offer my respectful obeisances to the Supreme Absolute
   Truth, Krishna, who is the well-wisher of the cows and the
   brahmanas as well as the living entities in general. I offer
   my repeated obeisances to Govinda [Krishna], who is the
   pleasure reservoir for all the senses.

After chanting these four mantras three times each, you can chant
the following mantra, called the *maha-mantra,* or great mantra,
several times.

*Hare Krishna, Hare Krishna, Krishna Krishna, Hare Hare
Hare Rama, Hare Rama, Rama Rama, Hare Hare*

One thing to remember is that Krishna is most interested in the love and devotion that went into preparing the offering. An important part of love and devotion to Krishna, or God, is freedom from habits and practices that cloud the mind and heart with material desires. The habits most detrimental to spiritual progress are meat-eating, gambling, intoxication, and illicit sex, and devotees of Krishna strictly avoid them. Spiritual purity is an essential ingredient in any offering to Krishna, so the more these four bad habits can be avoided, the purer one's consciousness will be when making the offering.

When the offering is completed, you and your family or guests can enjoy your meal. Food offered properly to Krishna undergoes a change—it becomes free of karma and infused with positive spiritual energy. The Sanskrit word for spiritual food offered to Krishna is *prasadam,* which means mercy.

Prasadam is especially wonderful because simply by eating it you can make spiritual advancement. It frees you from karma and lets you experience transcendental pleasure.

—Drutakarma Dasa, coauthor of
　*The Higher Taste: A Guide to Gourmet
　Vegetarian Cooking and a Karma-Free Diet*

Glossary of Spices And Special Ingredients

Anise Seed—A sweet spice that tastes like licorice. (Fennel seeds may be used as a substitute.)

Ajwan Seed—Has the fragrance of oregano and can be used as a substitute. Available at Indian specialty stores and in some supermarkets.

Asafetida—Gives a taste remimniscent of onion and garlic. Available at import and Indian specialty stores.

Atta (Chapati Flour)—A light-colored wheat flour available at Indian specialty stores.

Bay Leaves—Available in all grocery stores.

Black Cumin—Also called Black Jeera, it is available at import and Indian specialty stores. (Caraway seed may be substituted, but the flavor is not the same.

Besan—A flour made from chickpeas (also known as gram flour). Can be purchased at Indian specialty stores.

Cardamon—A sweet spice. The powder is available in most grocery stores. In Indian specialty stores it is found as a green or white pod containing small blackish seeds. The seeds may also be purchased separate.

Cashew—A sweetish nut. Comes whole or in pieces. Can be found in Indian specialty stores and health food stores.

Channa Dal—Halved garbanzo beans (chickpeas). Available in health food stores and organic food stores, as well as import and Indian specialty stores.

Chili Powder—A hot spice which is available at any grocery store. The Mexican Red is very hot and I use this one quite a lot.

Cinnamon—A sweet spice. Cinnamon stick is available at some grocery stores, but cinnamon powder is readily available. I prefer grinding the stick for a fresher fragrance and stronger taste. One stick is equal to ½ teaspoon powder.

Clove—This sweet spice is used in many of the recipes in this book. To make a powder, dry-roast and grind. Available at any grocery store.

Coriander (Cilantro)—Very versatile. The seeds are commonly used as a spice, wheras the fresh leaves and stems are used in cooking and as a garnish. (Parsley can be used as a substitute for coriander leaves.) To grow your own, plant in well-manured soil—6 inches apart for greens, 12 inches apart for seeds. The seeds can be ground into powder.

Cumin Seed—This spice is used frequently in Indian cooking. To make powder, dry-roast and grind. Available in any grocery store.

Curry Leaves—Also known as Dried Sweet Neem, it is available only at import or Indian specialty stores. If you cannot find it, it can be omitted.

Fennel Seed—Has a licorice flavor and can replace anise seeds. Available at any grocery store.

Fenugreek—A pungent spice available at any grocery store. Grind to make powder.

Garam Masala—A combination of various spices. Available in most grocery stores, but definitely in Indian specialty stores. To make it yourself, dry-roast separately 1 cup cumin seeds and 1 cup coriander seeds, then grind them into powder. Mix in ¼ cup cinnamon powder, ¼ cup nutmeg powder, and 3 tablespoons cardamon powder. Grind into powder 30 cloves. Mix well and store in an airtight jar.

Ginger Root—Used in many of the recipes in this book. Fresh ginger root, as well as powdered ginger is available in most grocery stores.

Karella (Bitter Melon)—A very bitter vegetable. It helps purify the blood, and is always taken before the meal in India. If there is a Chinatown or an oriental-produce store in your area, you can purchase these melons. Available canned in most Indian specialty stores, but the quality is not as good.

Mango Powder—Commonly known as amchor, it is available in Indian specialty stores.

Mung Dal—A high-protein Asian bean. The green variety can be found at many supermarkets and most health food stores. The yellow variety may be harder to find, except at Indian or Chinese specialty stores.

Mustard Seed—A very pungent spice. The black variety (most commonly used) is available at some grocery stores, and at all import and Indian specialty stores. Mustard powder is available everywhere.

Nutmeg—A common sweet spice, ground from the seeds of an evergreen tree indiginous to the Spice Islands. It can be purchased at any grocery store.

Peppercorns—Whole pepper seeds. When ground, you get black pepper powder. Available at any grocery store.

Pistacio—Small green nut, available primarily at Indian specialty stores. Some grocery stores sell unshelled pistacios, but don't get them salted, and you'll have to remove the shells.

Ponchphoron—This spice has to be made, but it's easy. Mix together ¼ cup anise or fennel seeds, ¼ cup fennugreek seeds, ¼ cup mustard seeds, ¼ cup cumin seeds, and ¼ cup black cumin or black jeera seeds. Store in an airtight jar.

Poppy Seed—Available at any grocery store. The best variety is light yellow, found at Indian specialty stores.

Saffron—Red, stringy sweet spice found at Indian specialty stores and some health food stores.

Sesame Seed—Whole sesame seeds are available at any grocery store.

Split Peas—Available at any grocery store.

Tamarind—Only available from import and Indian specialty stores. This spice is derived from the seed-pod, similar to carob, of a tropical tree, and is most commonly processed as a thick dark paste. It adds a wonderful tart flavor to vegetable dishes, and also makes a nice chutney.

Toora Dal—A type of bean grown in India. Only available from import and Indian specialty stores.

Turmeric—Yellow, pungent spice available as a powder at any grocery store. A better version is if you can get whole dried turmeric at an Indian store, soak it in water overnight, and grind it into a paste.

Urad Dal—Another popular bean from India. In some of the recipes in this book, it is used as a spice. It can be found at Indian specialty stores.